A Complete Bouldering Guide to

Joshua Tree

National Park

Robert Miramontes

I would like to dedicate this book to my mom.

Cover: Aron Couzens sending So High, photo: R. Miramontes

A complete bouldering guide to Joshua Tree National Park
©2003 R. Miramontes. All rights reserved. No part of this book may be reproduced in any manner without the written permission of the publisher.

Printed in the **U**nited **S**tates of **A**merica

ISBN: 0-9729373-0-7

Layout & Design by: R. Miramontes
Cover Design by: E.H. Graphix and R. Miramontes
Map Design and all uncredited photos by: R. Miramontes

Send comments, suggestions or any information in regards to bouldering in JTree to:
r.miramontes@worldnet.att.net

Printed, published and distributed by:
K. Daniels and Associates
14891 Sabre Lane
Huntington Beach CA 92647
(714) 434-9166

About K. Daniels & Associates

K D A has been printing catalogs and literature as well as distributing climbing equipment since 1991. A Complete Bouldering Guide To Joshua Tree National Park is our first climbing guide publication. Our goal is to create the highest quality guide books possible. If you have printing needs or are envisioning a climbing guide please contact us at:
kdanielsassociates@mindspring.com
(714) 434-9166

Thank you
K. Daniels & Associates

I would like to thank the following people;

Karin Sako, Kevin Daniels, Rob Mulligan, Brandi Proffitt Mulligan, Jon Browning, Greg Epperson, Kevin Powell, Randy Vogel, Scott Sanchez at webcrag.com, Alex"Dr.Topo's", Eric Jackson, Jack Hargis, Kevin Hovey, John Bachar, Dave & Margy Evans, Dale Bard, Kevin Thaw, John Jenkins, Craig Fry, my Aunt Frances and Gill, John Long, Mari Gingery for keeping track to begin with, all those trash talking fuggers on B.com, everyone who participated in the webcrag concensus, and any other poor saps that I talked into hiking all over BFE to find bouldering.

Warning:

Climbing is an inherently dangerous sport. None of the information contained within this guide is intended for instructional purposes. The user assumes all responsibility for the knowledge and experience required to boulder safely and to assess the potential dangers involved.

This guidebook is a compilation of information from many different sources. The author cannot guarantee that any of the information contained within it is accurate or reliable. Your use of this book indicates your assumption of the risk that it may contain errors and is an awknowledgement of your sole responsibility for your climbing safety.

Photo: R.Miramontes

Fade to White

What is Joshua Tree to me? Wandering across a sea of open desert, drifting off to some far away granite castle in search of hidden treasures. Peering giddily around the corner of every stone I come upon as if I were a child hunting for eggs on Easter morning. Is this an obsession?

Seeking out new problems in this vast metamorphic labyrinth is as much a part of my experience as the climbing itself; a spiritual journey across timeless landscapes in search of the simplest of answers. This is MY Joshua Tree, and within it exists an eerie beauty, of alien landscape, distorted figures and foreboding shadows. Even the trees stand twisted and gnarled, locked in some ethereal dance with the intoxicating waves of heat rising from the desert floor. Woven into this brilliant tapestry are Giant fortresses of granite; fantastic castles of golden stone rising hundreds of feet into the air, temples of light set against a deep blue sky.

Drifting across these dreamy scapes of Joshua Tree, one will occasionally come across a fine boulder problem, and for one crisp moment...

Everything becomes crystal clear.

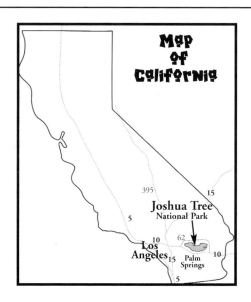

Map of California

Joshua Tree National Park

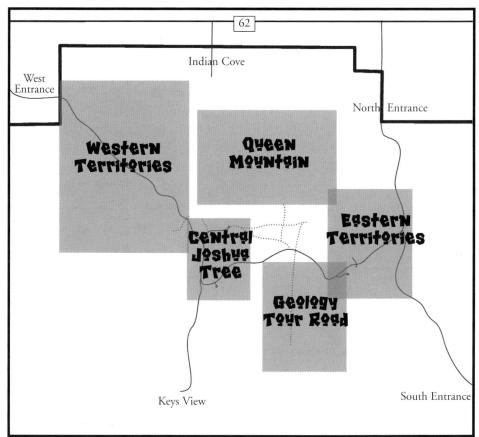

62

Indian Cove

West Entrance

North Entrance

Western Territories

Queen Mountain

Eastern Territories

Central Joshua Tree

Geology Tour Road

Keys View

South Entrance

Location

Joshua Tree National Park is located approximately 150 miles East of Los Angeles, and 35 miles North of Palm Springs in the high desert of Southern California. There are three entrances to the main park.

The West Entrance, located 5 miles South of the Town of Joshua Tree, is closest to all of the action and is the main portal for rock climbers into the park.

The North Entrance, which is a second option for climbers, is located 4 miles south of the town of 29 Palms.

The South Entrance is located 25 miles East of Palm Springs, off of the Interstate 10 at Chiriaco Summit. This entrance takes you on a long drive (40 miles) through portions of the park that most climbers never see. You gain a true sense of how big the Park is when you enter this way (currently 1240 square miles). There are several other portals into the park that don't connect to the main Park, one of these portals is Indian Cove, which is located 9 miles East of the Town of Joshua Tree on hwy. 62.

Park Fees

Park Main Number (760) 367-5500

Private Non-Commercial Vehicles(for a 7-day pass)	$10.00
Individual Entry (on bike or on foot)	$5.00
Annual Park Pass (season)	$25.00
Gold Access Passport (blind/permanently disabled)	Free (lifetime)
Golden Age Passport (one-time fee, lifetime)	$10.00
Golden Eagle Passport (annual, good in all NP's)	$50.00

Park Campground Beta

Campground Reservations (800) 365-CAMP (-2267)

Belle	18 sites @ 3,800 ft./No Fee
Black Rock	100 sites @ 4,000 ft./Water/Flushing toilets/$12.00
Cottonwood	62 sites, 3 group sites @ 3,000 ft./Water/Flushing toilets/ $10.00
Hidden Valley	39 sites @ 4,200 ft./No Fee
Indian Cove	101 sites, 13 group sites @ 3,200 ft./$10
Jumbo Rock	125 sites @ 4,400 ft./No Fee
Ryan	31 sites @ 4,300 ft./No Fee
Sheep Pass	6 group sites @ 4,500 ft./No Fee
White Tank	15 sites @ 3,800 ft./No Fee

Other Lodging

High Desert Motel   61310 29 Palms Hwy. (Hwy. 62), Joshua Tree, CA 92252 (760) 366-1978
Joshua Tree Inn (B & B)   61259 29 Palms Hwy. (Hwy. 62), Joshua Tree, CA 92252 (760) 366-1188
Safari Motor Inn   61959 29 Palms Hwy. (Hwy. 62), Joshua Tree, CA 92252 (760) 366-1113

Eats

Country Kitchen   61768 29 Palms Hwy., Joshua Tree, CA 92252 (760) 366-8988
Crossroads Café & Tavern   61715 29 Palms Hwy., Joshua Tree, CA 92252

Sam's Pizza & Subs   61380 29 Palms Hwy., Joshua Tree, CA 92252 (760) 366-9511

Gear & Goodies

Coyote Corner   6535 Park Blvd., Joshua Tree, CA 92252
(760) 366-9683
Nomad Ventures   61795 29 Palms Hwy., Joshua Tree, CA 92252
(760) 366-4684
Park Center   6554 Park Blvd., Joshua Tree, CA 92252
(760) 366-3448

Food Stores

Joshua Tree Health Foods   61693 29 Palms Hwy., Joshua Tree, CA
92252 (760) 366-7489
Sue's Health Foods   56475 29 Palms Hwy., Joshua Tree, CA
92252 (760) 365-1158

Climate

If you asked me personally, I'd tell you that Josh is climbable all year round, but most people think I'm crazy when I tell them that I climb there in the summer. Generally, fall, winter and spring are considered the seasons for climbing in J-Tree. Temps average between 50-80°F during these seasons. Nights in the winter can get down into the low 30's. Weather in JT tends to be fair, with the only real concern being high winds that can be unbearably cold and are notorious for turning clear blue sky days into sight seeing trips from the car. Temps in the summer average from 90-105°F , but it's not uncommon to have sub 90° days...no seriously!

When I started this project, I had big hopes of uncovering the rich and colorful history gleaned from generations of pioneers who have climbed in Joshua Tree. It quickly became apparent that this was not going to be an easy task. Much of the "Golden Era" First Ascent information is probably forgotten or lost forever. Often times, the routes were not taken that seriously, let alone the bouldering. This is very unfortunate because with the likes of Royal Robbins, T.M.Herbert, Tom Frost and other Yosemite pioneers back in the 1950's "practicing" for the "real stuff" in the Park, one can imagine that they must have climbed on the many boulders strewn throughout the campgrounds. The first guidebook for climbing in Joshua Tree, published in 1971, has a picture of Ken Wolf bouldering the Old Triangle Classic.

It was'nt until the 70's that people began to take bouldering seriously enough to keep track of the problems. John Long, John Yablonski, Lynn Hill and John Bachar were some of the first to embrace this new fascination. Back in a time when sit starts were referred to as "Yabo" starts, First Ascent's (such as Saturday Night Live) were bagged shit faced in the middle of the night and taller always meant better. It was mainly Bachar though, pushing all the limits - planet X, So High, Pumping Monzonite, Central Scrutinizer (onsight), All Washed Up and Caveman...all his vision.

Many other masters have left their footprints in the golden sand. Jerry Moffat, Kevin Powell, Darrell Hensel, Dale Bard, Johnny Woodward, Ron Kauk, Dean Fidelman, Charles Cole, Craig Fry, Skip Guerin, Mike Lechlinski, Mari Gingery, Mike Paul, Russ Walling, Dick Cilley, and many others, throughout the decades, wandered across the nomadic plains and through the mysterious landscapes of Joshua Tree in search of proud bouldering.

Even today curious adventurers strike out in search of hidden gems tucked away in monzogranite mazes or high on a rocky monolith. Some of these modern-day stonemasters include Scott Cozgrove, Matt Beebe, Kevin Daniels, Eric Jackson, Rob Mulligan, Rico Miledi, myself and many others that we may never know about. Even the legendary Fred Nicole has left us a few gems!

Photo: K.Powell

Lynn Hill on the Manx Boulder

Impact Issues

Joshua tree is a highly fragile wilderness environment. Climbers visiting the park should strive to keep their impact to a absolute minimum. Upon entering the park for the first time, I would recommend obtaining a visitors guide and familiarize yourselves with the parks "Rules and Regulations". There are rangers out here, and they bust people often!

Chalk use should be kept to a minimal. If you must use tick marks, please clean them off before leaving the area. Chalk stripes or throwing chalk balls at high holds is unacceptable. Chiseling rock, altering landing areas, or clearing away foliage is illegal and strictly forbidden. Climbing within 50 feet of native rock art is also illegal. All wildlife in Joshua Tree is protected and should not be disturbed.

Several of the new areas described in this guide exist in pristine wilderness where hardly a trace of human impact can be found. When climbing at The Underground, Queen Mountain, Geology Tour Road or Valley of the Kings, extreme care should be taken to "leave no trace".

Ratings

This guide utilizes the V-scale, which originated at Hueco Tanks, and has since become the standard for rating boulder problems in the U.S.. Much effort was made to achieve a consensus for the grades, however Josh has a reputation for being sandbagged. Problems are rated based on the easiest beta. Due to the sometimes featureless qualities of the rock, many problems are height dependant.

Quality

The quality of a Boulder problem is highly subjective and everyones opinion may vary. The "star system" in this guide was based on these factors;

Rock quality: Probably the most influential factor.

Purity of line: How obvious is the line. All 5 star problems are striking lines.

Movement: Does the problem have interesting, unusual or fun moves?

U.S.	French	YDS	B System
.9	5+	5.9	.9
v0	6a	5.10	.10
v1			.10+
v2	6a+	5.11	.11
	6b		
v3	6b+		.11+
v4	6c		B1-
	6c+	5.12	
v5	7a		B1
v6	7a+		B1+
v7	7b		B2-
v8	7b+	5.13	B2
v9	7c		
v10	7c+		
v11	8a		
v12	8a+	5.14	
v13	8b		

Conversion Chart

Height: Whether you like tall problems or not, they are always a little bit sweeter when you bag the send.

Bad landings, short problems, or unusually painful climbing can all have a negative affect.

Danger

Problems that are tall, or have bad landings, will be noted with an "**R**"(unusual risk of injury) or "**X**"(high risk, serious injury). I will attempt to list all the problems over 15 feet, and note any unusual fall potential. All bouldering can be potentially dangerous, and typical hazards will not be specifically addressed.

About GPS

This book utilizes GPS to aid in locating boulders. GPS is not 100% accurate and should not be considered as such, however it is accurate enough to put you close to hard to find problems. Average accuracy is to within 30 feet. Steep canyon walls and clouds may significantly reduce signal reception.

Maps

All the maps contained in this book are based on USGS survey maps, and should be accurate down to the formations. The boulders shown are approximations, and the boulders that have problems on them are usually enlarged for detail. All maps are oriented as North being towards the top of the page, except in the case of Stonehenge and Headstone, which were turned for easier referencing.

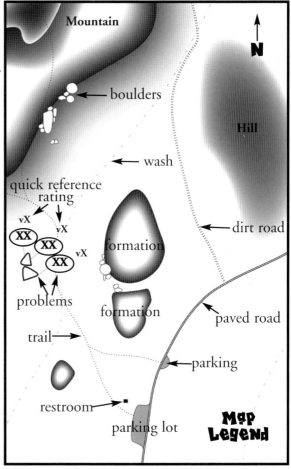

Mountain

N

boulders

Hill

wash

quick reference rating

vX

vX

XX

XX

vX

XX

formation

dirt road

problems

formation

paved road

trail

parking

restroom

Map Legend

parking lot

Photo: R.Miramontes

Jonathan Wright on Alexandria

Western Territories

This section covers the Western most bouldering areas of the park. From the West Entrance, traveling East on Park Boulevard, the Embryo Boulders are encountered first(1.5 mi.), followed by the Miledi Boulders (2.0 mi.). Further down on the left, in front of the boulder covered hill "Negropolis" you will find The Chocolate Boulders (3.4 mi.). On the right, across the valley is Quail Mountain (5813'), the highest mountain in Joshua Tree. Quail Springs picnic area aka: Trashcan Rock(5.8 mi.), and Afpa Rock across the road are the final areas covered.

© G. Epperson

Kevin Daniels on Act of Contrition

Chapter

1

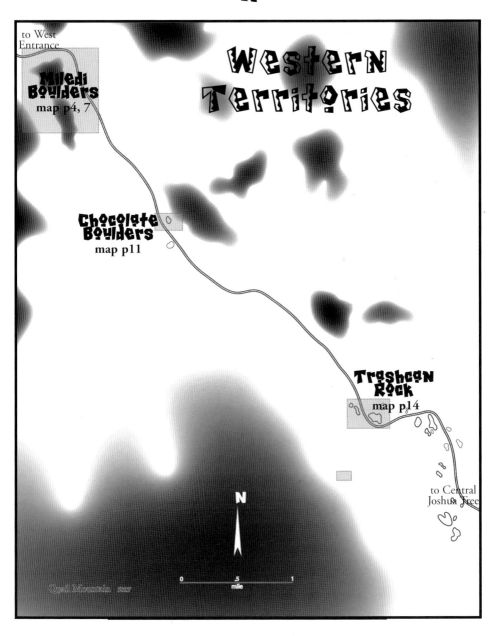

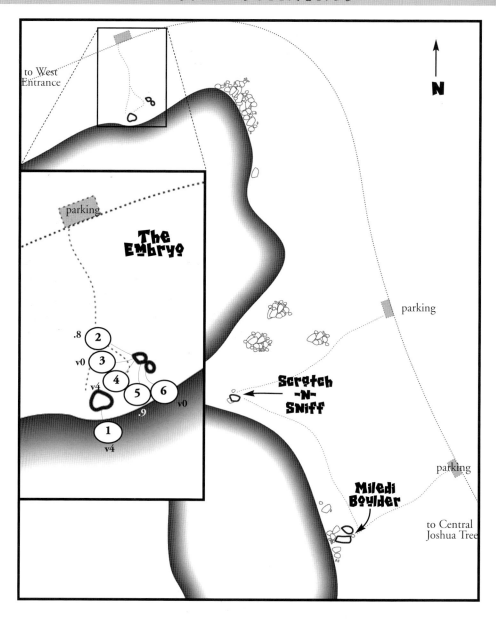

1 The Embryo V4
2 Primer .8
3 Blip Trip V0

4 Quiff V4
5 Blip .9
6 Unnamed V0

Embryo Boulder (GPS = N34° 04.842 W116° 14.757)
From the West Entrance, travel 1.5 miles to a turnout on the left, walk to the obvious boulders on the right at the base of the hill. Map p4

**1 The Embryo V4 ** Start at a diagonal rail, then stem up the smooth concave face. This problem is easier if you are tall.

Blip Boulder Map p4

2 Primer .8 Sit start at a diagonal crack and climb left up to a knobby arête.

3 Blip Trip V0 Start primer but traverse right at a horizontal crack. Finish up the right arête.

4 Quiff V4 Sit start at the diagonal crack, move right to a blunt arête with a seam, finish up the arête.

5 Blip .9 Hand traverse left on the sloping top of the boulder, then mantel over at the upper arête.

6 Unnamed V0 Start on a low jug and dyno right to a knobby bucket.

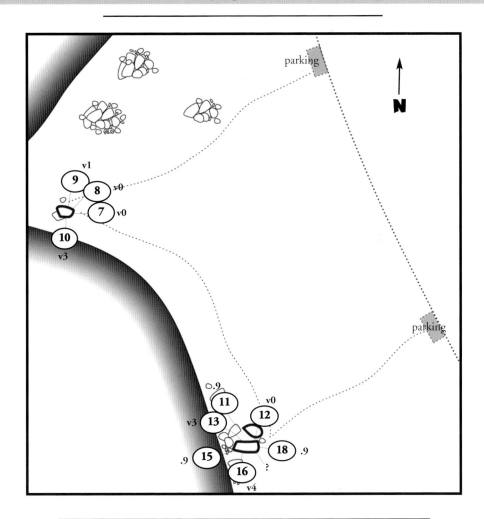

7 Don't Puss V0-
8 Scratch Arete V0
9 Scratch-n-Sniff V1
10 Something for Nothing V3
11 Unnamed .9
12 Easy Bones V0 R

13 Miledi V3 R ***
14 Miledi (sit) V5 R ***
15 Warm-Down .9
16 K.D. Supreme V4 ***
17 K.D. Supreme (sit) V6 ***
18 Hoffmans Highman .9 R

Miledi Boulders

From West Entrance, go 2.0 miles to turnout on the right, Scratch-n-Sniff is in the notch between the two hills, and the Miledi Boulder is at the base of the hill, 200 yds left of the notch. Map p7

Scratch-N-Sniff Boulder (GPS = 34° 04.590 W116° 14.591) Map p7

7 Don't Puss V0- Mantel over on jugs, then tackle the friction face above.

8 Scratch Arête V0 Grainy buckets to a rounded arête with a nice lip on it.

9 Scratch-n-Sniff V1 Climb hollow plates in the center of a vertical face. No arête.

10 Something for Nothing V3 Grainy crimps on a steep slab.

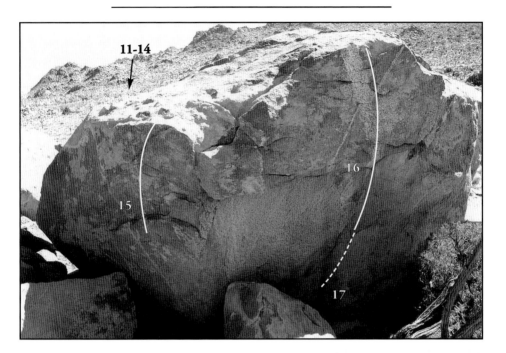

Miledi Boulder (GPS = N34° 04.528 W116° 14.522) Map p7

11 Unnamed .9 Grainy jugs next to an arête.

12 Easy Bones V0 R Climb the dihedral/crack line to jugs.

13 Miledi V3 R * Lieback a giant flake in vertical terrain, up to a committing friction move high up.

14 Miledi (sit) V5 R * Sit start and climb squatty moves under the flake, moving right to access the lieback flake.

15 Warm-down .9 Ledges and buckets with a bad landing.

16 K.D. Supreme V4 * Start at a vertical seam and climb up to an edge and sidepulls on overhanging rock, finishing with knobs.

17 K.D. Supreme (sit) V6 * Sit start and lieback the thin seam up to the regular start.

18 Hoffmans Highman .9 R Step off a large boulder to a juggy crack that slabs out towards the top. Bad landing.

Chocolate
Boulders

From the West Entrance go 3.4 miles to a turnout on the right. Cross the road and approach the large boulder covered hill (Negropolis), around the right side of a small hill. These dark boulders are hidden between these two hills. Map p3, 11

19 Swinging Richard Direct V2 *
20 Swinging Richard V4 ***
21 Smoothie .9

22 Lumpy .7
23 Mini-Slab .9
24 Mini-Arete .7

Chocolate

Bishops

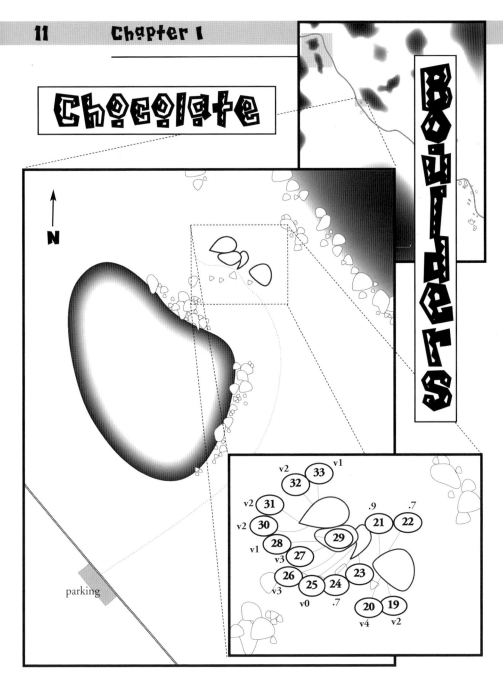

Chocolate 1 The first of three large brown boulders. Map p11
19 Swinging Richard Direct V2 * Start at the bucket and move up the arête to knobs.
20 Swinging Richard V4 *** Start on the bucket on the right and climb the overhung, diagonal crack with jugs every 4 feet or so, turn the lip or finish up the arête.
21 Smoothie .9 Edging up a smooth patina slab.
22 Lumpy .7 Mantel start to a juggy crack.

Chocolate Chip A small broken shard of rock. Map p11
23 Mini-Slab .9 A short edging problem up the center of the face.
24 Mini-Arête .7 A short, low angle, knobby arête.

Chocolate 2 (GPS = N34° 03.755 W116° 13.584) The middle boulder. Map p11
25 Tush V0- * Sit start in a small alcove, then climb out the short overhang via the crack formed by the two boulders.
26 Bodacious V3 * Start at a rounded arête, thin edges move you left and up on slightly less than vertical stone. Low start is v6.
27 Thin Face V3 Climb micro-edges up the center face joining Bodacious at the top.
28 Bodacious Rail V1 * Start on the left side of the face, and traverse right along the lippy rail to join with Bodacious at the top.
29 Sinfully Delicious .9 * Slab move up to patina.

Chocolate 3 The last boulder in the circuit. Map p11
30 Attractive Brunette Throw V2 * Start on low flakes, move left to the arête, then chuck to the bucket up right.
31 Attractive Brunette V2 * Sit start at a low jug and send the lumpy arête.
32 Torpedo V2 * Awkward moves on a slab.
33 Stinger V1 More slab funk.

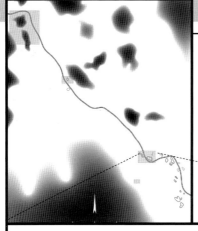

Trashcan / Afpa Rock

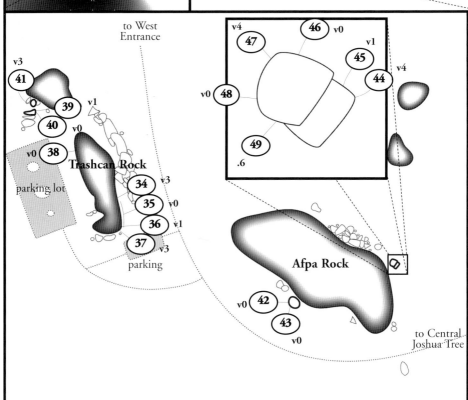

34 The Butterfly Crack V3 R ***
35 Gripper Traverse V0+ *
36 Ripper V2 **
37 Whipper V3/4
38 Block Problem V0-
39 Unnamed V1
40 Unnamed V0
41 Simpson Slap V3

42 Boulder Crack V0 R **
43 Boulder Face V0
44 Blort V4 *
45 Elbow Grease V1 *
46 Church of the Jack Lord V0- R *
47 Bubblebutt V4 *
48 Sidestep V0
49 Descent Route .6

From
the West Entrance, travel 5.8 miles to a rock formation on the right with a large parking lot and restroom facilities. Map p3, 14

Trashcan Rock (GPS = N34° 02.415 W116° 11.816) The East Face of the formation, 20 ft. from the parking lot. Map p14.

34 The Butterfly Crack V3 R * ** Climb a clean finger crack on a vertical wall, up to buckets. Downclimb and jump, or topout on .9 jugs (30 ft).

35 Gripper Traverse V0+ * A slightly overhung 30 ft. traverse with jugs, slopers, and incut crimps.

36 Ripper V2 ** Start on low jugs, fire the overhang and cross into the crack. Downclimb and jump or topout on .7 flaring crack (30 ft.).

37 Whipper V3/4 Mantel onto the rotten flake, friction up the grainy slab, then finish with a 30 ft. tall flaring crack (.7). Sounds like fun huh?

38 Block Problem V0- Climb the stairstep dike up the steep slab.

Forgotten Boulders Map p14.

39 Unnamed V1 Big moves on big, grainy pinches with an uneven landing.
40 Unnamed V0 A short, overhanging crack with jugs.
41 Simpson Slap V3 Bearhug the blunt arête.

Afpa Rock

Located on the left, across the street from Trashcan Rock (5.8 mi.). Boulder Crack faces the road, while Broken Boulder is on the backside. Map p14

Boulder Boulder (GPS = N34° 02.366 W116° 11.700) Located directly in front of the Afpa formation.

**42 Boulder Crack V0 R ** ** A juggy overhanging jam crack leads to a high dihedral.
43 Boulder Face V0 R Start at boulder crack, but take the right horizontal crack around the corner and over on knobs.

Broken Boulder (GPS = N34° 02.409 W116° 11.627) This boulder is on the back side of the Afpa formation. Map p14.

44 Blort V4 * Hug the blunt arête with tricky slopers.

45 Elbow Grease V1 * Mantel onto the shelf, then do a long reach for the lip.

46 Church of the Jack Lord V0- R * Climb up and onto a dark, round, precarious patina patch, then strike out right on a committing face 20 ft. up.

47 Bubblebutt V4 * Jump to slopers on a high slab over a roof, then perform a technical mantel.

48 Sidestep V0 Step off of a boulder, then move left and up on nice patina.

49 Descent Route .6 The crack line on the back of the boulder.

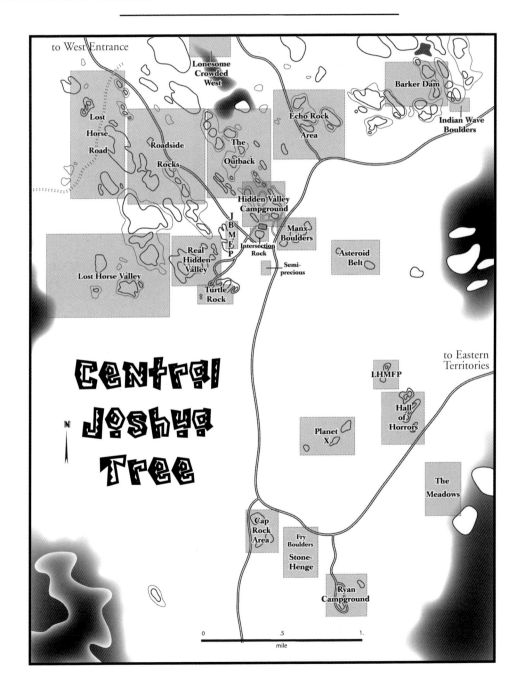

to West Entrance

Lonesome
Crowded
West

Barker Dam

Lost
Horse
Road

Roadside

Rocks

The
Outback

Echo Rock
Area

Indian Wave
Boulders

Hidden Valley
Campground

J
B
M
E
P

Manx
Boulders

Intersection
Rock

Real
Hidden
Valley

Semi-
precious

Asteroid
Belt

Lost Horse Valley

Turtle
Rock

to Eastern
Territories

N

LHMFP

Central
Joshua
Tree

Hall
of
Horrors

Planet
X

The
Meadows

Cap
Rock
Area

Fry
Boulders

Stone-
Henge

Ryan
Campground

0   .5   1.
mile

Central Joshua Tree

Central Joshua Tree

As our journey takes us into the heart of Joshua Tree, the desert unfurls a bizarre playground of stone, the setting for lifetimes of climbing. This is where the majority of all climbing in Joshua Tree can be found. Sixteen chapters are covered in this section, starting with the Lost Horse Area, moving through the Hidden Valley Campground, up into the Barker Dam Area, and finally working down to Cap Rock, Ryan Campground, and Hall of Horrors. Virtually all of the well known classics are here.

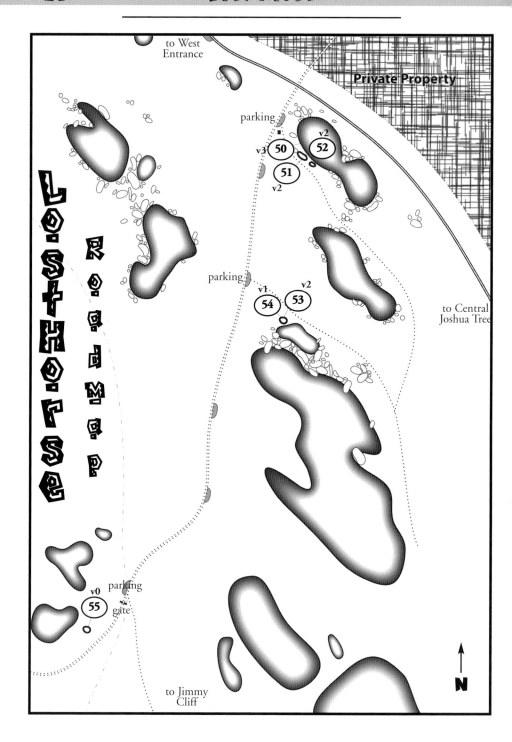

Chapter 2

Lost Horse

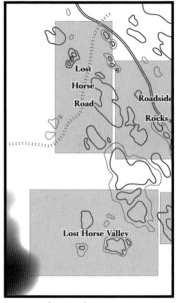

Lost Horse Road

Highlights in this area include the photo ops on Aguille de Joshua Tree, the brutal overhanging Kevitation Crack and the overhanging arete Penguins in Bondage. From the West Entrance travel 7.4 miles to a junction, turn right (turning left is private property, please do not enter this area), the bouldering is scattered along the roadside. There are restroom facilities at the junction. Map p18, 20

Jimmy Cliff

Drive down the dirt road until you reach a gate (service road), park here and walk SE along the formations, after about .25 mile Aguille de Joshua can be seen, angle right and walk another 200 yds, Penguins area is at the base of the Jimmy Cliff formation. The alternate approach is to park at Real Hidden Valley and walk S SW along the formations, angling West. After .25 mile the steep crack Kevitation (SW facing) can be seen on the right, 20 feet up at the base of the formation. Angle left and walk to the base of the Jimmy Cliff formation. Map p18, 24

50 Bandini Mountain V3
51 The Bardini Crack V2 **
52 Cornholio V2

53 Velveeta V2
54 Cheeze Whiz V1
55 Big Bud V0 R

Blas Bimmer Boulder (GPS = N34° 01.671 W116° 10.725) Park just after turning onto the dirt road, the boulder is 100 ft. to the right, on the backside of the formation. Map p20

50 Bandini Mountain V3 Start at a diagonal crack, then move left to slopers and climb into the scoop.

51 The Bardini Crack (aka; Blas Bimmer) V2 ** A slightly overhanging thin crack on a pocketed face.

52 Cornholio V2 Sit start at a low jug, climb a short overhang to a pocket, then roll over onto the slab.

Cheese Boulder

(GPS = N34° 01.536 W116° 10.755) Park at the second turnout and walk East for 150 ft, left of the formation. Map p20

53 Velvetta V2 Start at a high sidepull on a vertical wall and huck for the top.

54 Cheese Whiz V1 Grainy sidepull edges through a scoop.

Big Bud (GPS = N34° 01.207 W116° 10.989) Park at the gate turnout, walk down the service road for 100 yds, the boulder is 30 ft. off the road on the left. Map p20

55 Big Bud V0 R * Edges, dishes, and slopers up a 22 ft. tall less-than-vertical face. Bad landing.

Jimmy Cliff

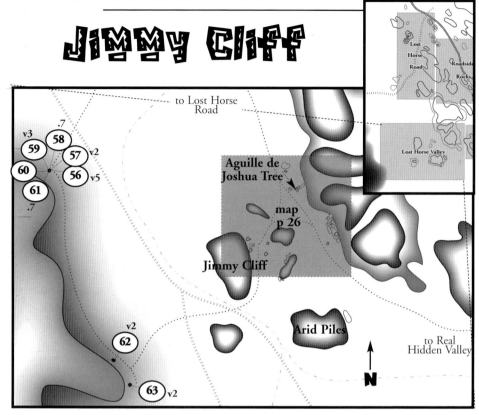

56 Yabaho Dyno V5 **
57 Yabaho Right V2
58 Unnamed .7
59 Dinky Doinks V3

60 Yabo Nation V2
61 Unnamed .7
62 Trifle V2
63 The Final Bulge V2

Yabo Boulder (GPS = N34° 00.978 W116° 11.317) Park at the gate and walk South across the desert for .5 mile, or walk the service road around and back to the base of the mountain. The boulder is located along the base of the mountain. Map p24

**56 Yabaho Dyno V5 ** ** Go up and left off the undercling to a vertical patina rail, finishing with a huge double dyno for the top.

57 Yabaho Right V2 * Climb right off the hollow undercling to a hollow sidepull plate, finishing with a minor toss for the lip.

58 Unnamed .7 Climb the ramp/arete up to jugs.

59 Dinky Doinks V3 Hollow plates and grainy crimps over a small bulge, a hard low start exists.

60 Yabo Nation V2 Hollow plates and grainy crimps over a bulge, a much harder low start exists.

61 Unnamed .7 A low ramp up to plates and small jugs over a bulge.

Trifle greg Walk .25 mile past Yabo Boulder along the base of the mountain. Map p24

62 Trifle V2 Thin edges and seams on a vertical patina face.

63 The Final Bulge V2 A right slanting under a roof/bulge to jugs.

Aguille de Joshua Tree (GPS = N34° 00.864 W116° 10.681) Located up near the formation on the desert floor, 100 yds. south of a large boulder with lead bolts. Dysfunction is at the base of this boulder. Map p26

64 Dysfunction V1 A thin lieback seam with high feet on a vertical face.

65 Aguille de Joshua Tree .6 X * Climb the 20 ft. shard of granite. The summit is about 2 ft. by 2 ft. and about 30 ft tall on one side, horrible landing.

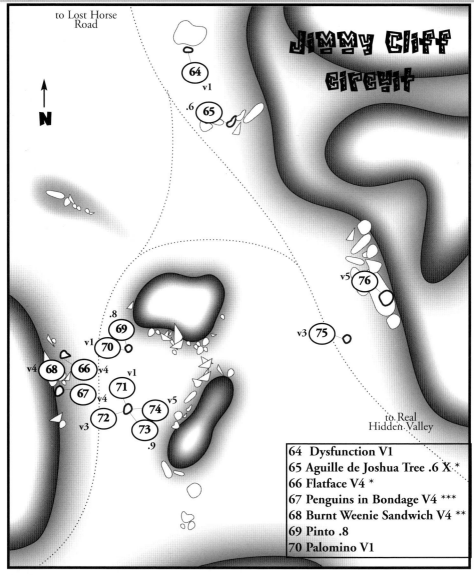

to Lost Horse Road

N

JiMMy Cliff Cireuit

64
v1

.6 65

v5 76

.8
69
v1 70
v4 68 66 v4 v1
67 71
v4
72 74 v5
v3 73
.9

v3 75

to Real Hidden Valley

64	**Dysfunction V1**
65	**Aguille de Joshua Tree .6 X ***
66	**Flatface V4 ***
67	**Penguins in Bondage V4 *****
68	**Burnt Weenie Sandwich V4 ****
69	**Pinto .8**
70	**Palomino V1**

71 Bob V1   **74 Spleef V5**
72 Ziggy V3   **75 The Unmentionable V3**
73 Rita .9   **76 Kevitation V5 *****

---

66 Flatface V4 * A slightly overhanging, smooth patina face with thin edges.

Penguins Boulder Map p26
67 Penguins in Bondage V4 *** Start at finger slots/cracks 2 ft. in from

the arête, send the cruxy overhanging arête, moving right to a triangular hole, then up to jugs. 16 ft. tall with a menacing rock at the crux.

68 Burnt Weenie Sandwich V4 ** Climb the shorter right arête with thin crimps.

69 Pinto .8 A juggy slab with black lichen.

70 Palomino V1 Pull over off a high sloping dish.

Marley Boulder (GPS = N34° 00.740 W116° 10.740) Map p26

71 Bob V1 A short overhang with a diagonal seam and patina.

72 Ziggy V3 Use a cheatstone to get to a high flake on a short overhung face.

73 Rita .9 Balancy moves up black fins on a slab.

74 Spleef V5 Sit start and climb a scooped out section of overhang up and right to a crack and over.

The Unmentionable

From the parking lot walk South, past Saturday Night Live, around the formation for approx. 600 yds. as it bends to the West (do not enter any canyons), The Unmentionable is under a low roof on the west side of the boulder, Kevitation is visible 30 ft. up in the formation. Map p26

75 The Unmentionable V3
Sit start under a short overhang and boulderout the steep crack/rail.

Mayville Boulder

(GPS = N34° 00.735 W116° 10.533) Follow the directions

to The Unmentionable, Kevitation is the obvious crack on the Southwest side of the large boulder, perched on a ledge 30 ft. up in the rocks. Map p26

76 Kevitation V5 *** Sit start and climb the wide crack in the 45° wall, turn the scary lip and finish up the easy low angle crack. Originally climbed as a toprope.

Chapter 3

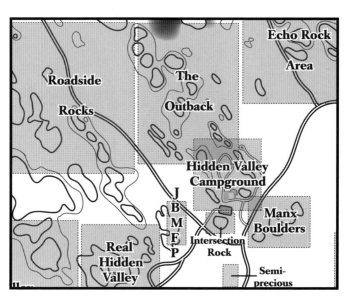

Rocks

Roadside Rocks

As you enter this area, the rock formations become much denser. Much of the land to the left (North) of the road is private property, please do not enter this area. All of the bouldering is found on the South side of the road. Map p18, 30

Turnout 1 From the West Entrance, travel 7.8 miles to a large parking lot. Restrooms can be found at this location. Many lead climbs can also be found in this area.

Turnout 2 From the West Entrance, travel 8.0 miles to a turnout on the right.

Turnout 3 From the West Entrance, travel 8.4 miles to a turnout on the right. This is the main area of Roadside Rocks.

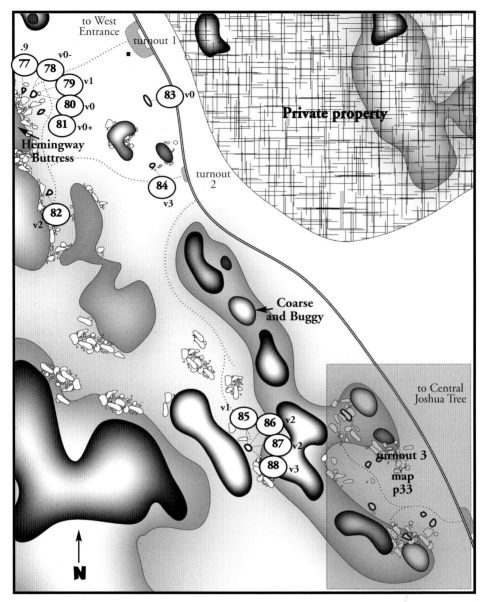

77 Unknown .9
78 Unknown V0- *
79 Unknown V1 *
80 Unknown V0
81 The Undertaker V0+ *
82 Sheiznik V2

83 Dead Pinyon Crack V0
84 Pepboys Problem V3 *
85 Enter the Melon V1
86 Classic Melon V2
87 Melonizer V2
88 Mini-Melon V3

Hemingway Boulders

(GPS = N 34° 01.436 W116° 10.624) These boulders are located at the base of Hemingway Buttress. Map p30

77 Unknown .9 Smear and hop up to a large flake.

78 Unknown V0- * Start at a low jug and the arete, up to a large flake.

79 Unknown V1 * Start at thin edges (avoid the loose plate) sidepull up to high edges.

80 Unknown V0 Start at a sloper/shelf and lieback the arete.

Undertaker

50 ft. left of Hemingway Boulders. Map p30

81 The Undertaker V0+ * Start at low incuts, chuck for the arete, then power the bulge.

Sheiznik

Located at the base of the next formation to the left known as the Dairy Queen Wall. Map p30

82 Sheiznik V2 Grainy crimps and a sloper/arete.

Pinyon Rock (GPS = N34° 01.403 W116°10.478)
Located between turnouts 1 and 2, 100 ft.
from the road. Map p30

83 Dead Pinyon Crack V0 ** R Climbs a
sweet tips lieback up to sweeeeeeet jams 20
ft. up.

The Milepost (GPS = N34° 01.348 W116°
10.417) 50 ft. west of turnout 2. Map p30

84 Pepboys Problem V3 * Climb a short,
knobby crack to a sloper mantel.

Melon Boulder (GPS = N34 ° 01.068 W116°
10.336) From turnout 2 walk behind the
formation just to the left, follow an old miners
road through the canyon. When it opens up
stay left until the canyon pinches off, the
boulder is located behind a tree on the right
side of the wash. Map p30

85 Enter the Melon V1* Small edges up and
right to sweet patina knobs.

86 Classic Melon V2 ** Climbs a blunt arete
with slopers, a cool hueco and tite knobs.

87 Melonizer V2* Start at a
black pinch and climb a
dished out vert. face with
technical moves.

88 Mini-Melon V3 Start at a
high diagonal seam, power
over the short face on
slopers.

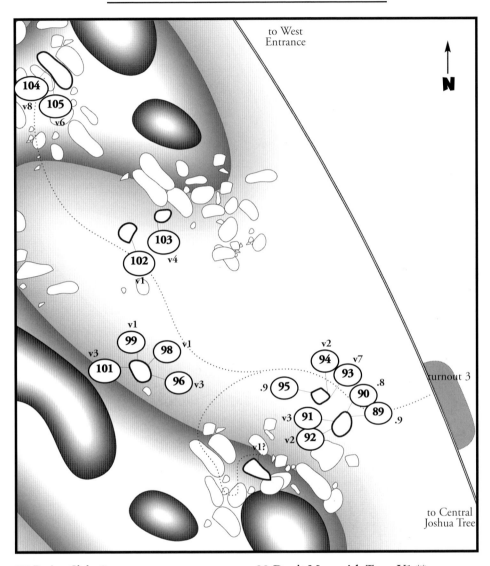

89 Patina Slab .9
90 Chunkers .8 **
91 Weasel World (left exit) V3
92 Weasel World V2
93 Trance V7
94 Lip Service V2 **
95 Unnamed .9
96 Western Roll V3 *
97 Western Roll (sit) V5 **

98 Don't Mess with Texas V1 **
99 Border Patrol V1
100 Border Patrol (sit) V6 *
101 La Migra V3 **
102 Pacifier V1 *
103 The Nostril V4
104 Plank Walk V8 **
105 Lost at Sea V6

Chunky Boulder Map p33

89 Patina Slab .9 Edge straight up the center of the face.

90 Chunkers .8 ** An overhanging arête with jugs.

91 Weasel World (left exit) V3 Start at a high sidepull, then go left to slopers.

92 Weasel World V2 Start at a high sidepull and go straight up.

Trance Stone (GPS = N34° 01.108 W116° 10.137) Map p33

93 Trance V7 Climb the sharp arête all the way out, off routing the rail on the right (Lip Service).

94 Lip Service V2 ** Start pinching the clean, overhanging arête, and fire right to a sweet rail.

95 Unnamed .9 Lieback and mantel the shallow huecos.

Texas Boulder (GPS = N34° 01.088 W116° 10.189) The obvious large boulder up against the formation, back in the alcove. Map p33

96 Western Roll V3 * Start on cranky little sidepulls on a slight overhang, and crank to a standard josh mantel.

97 Western Roll (sit) V5 ** This start is harder than it looks! Start anywhere on the low shelf, then move into the regular start.

98 Don't Mess with Texas V1 ** Sit start at a bucket, then climb friendly incut flakes and sidepulls on a slight overhang.

99 Border Patrol V1 Start at a horizontal crack with incuts and perform a textbook mantel.

100 Border Patrol (sit) V6 * Sit start at a low horizontal crack with incuts and no feet, then crank up to the regular start.

101 La Migra V3 ** Cool problem! Stem into an overhanging bowl from the right, then toss for buckets over the top.

Nostril Boulder (GPS = N34° 01.110 W116° 10.224)These two problems are located in the alcove on the right side. Map p33

102 Pacifier V1 * A smooth brown, slabby arête with a thin crack in it.

103 The Nostril V4 Start at an undercling/hole and pimp crystals on the slab above.

The Deck (GPS = N34° 01.119 W116°10.269) Walk past Pacifier and to the back of the alcove, scramble up the small notch between the hills. This short overhanging cliff band is on the right side, on the hill. Map p33

104 Plank Walk V8 ** Sit start at a low fin and lieback the way steep thin crack. Bad landing.

105 Lost at Sea V6 Sit start as low as possible on the overhanging jam crack, climb up to a black sloping knob, then move left into a rotten crack. Poor landing area.

Chapter 4

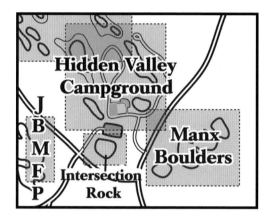

JBMFP

One of the many circuits masterminded by John Bachar, the area testpiece JBMFP pays homage to his legacy. Here you can find the balancy, thin JBMFP, the tall clean lieback False Up 20 and many short steep power problems.

The parking for this area is at Intersection Rock. From the West Entrance, travel 8.8 miles to the intersection. The JBMFP boulders are on the right just before the intersection. Turn left at the intersection and park in the large parking lot (restroom facilities can be found here), walk back across the road(SW). The boulders are scattered across the base of the formation. Map p18, 38

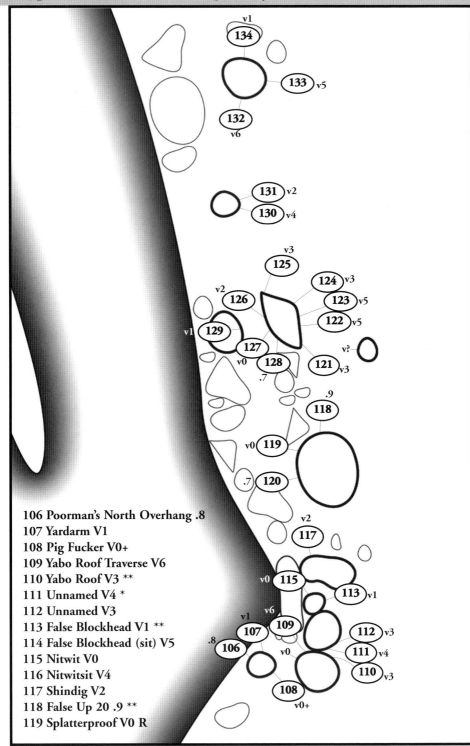

106 Poorman's North Overhang .8
107 Yardarm V1
108 Pig Fucker V0+
109 Yabo Roof Traverse V6
110 Yabo Roof V3 **
111 Unnamed V4 *
112 Unnamed V3
113 False Blockhead V1 **
114 False Blockhead (sit) V5
115 Nitwit V0
116 Nitwitsit V4
117 Shindig V2
118 False Up 20 .9 **
119 Splatterproof V0 R

120 Descent Crack .7
121 True Grit V3/4 **
122 JBMFP V5 ****
123 Razarium V5 **
124 Two Stroke V3 *
125 Lechlinski Corner V3 **
126 Hensel Face V2
127 Penny Pincher V0-

128 Descent Route .7
129 Death Series V1
130 Browning Arete V4
131 Slick Willie V2 *
132 Skip's Arete V6
133 The Terminator V5
134 English Leather V1

Yardarm Boulder Map p38

106 Poormans North Overhang .8 Climb dishes up to a roof, then exit up a crack on the right.

107 Yardarm V1 A vertical face with a slot midway.

108 Pig Fucker V0+ A contender for the worst problem in Josh. Grope an overhanging groove with sloping huecos on crumbling, grainy rock. Mantel over with a bush in your face.

Yabo Roof (GPS = N34° 00.883 W116° 09.945) Map p38

109 Yabo Roof Traverse V6 Sit start at crack slots, traverse left 10 feet, then mantel the same as yabo roof.

110 Yabo Roof V3 ** Sit start under a roof at semi-jugs, toss to the sharp lip, then do a cool mantel.

111 Unnamed V4 * Sit start under the roof on a big flake, fire up to slopers, then crawl through a tree to finish.

112 Unnamed V3 Lean off of diagonal cracks, do a big move to a sloper, then turn the corner and crawl through the tree.

Blockhead Map p38

113 False Blockhead V1 ** Start on an incut rail, chuck big for a sloper, then grovel straight over the bulge.

114 False Blockhead (sit) V5 Thin plates on a small overhang.

115 Nitwit V0 Climb buckets and hollow plates above a small overhang.

116 Nitwitsit V4 Sit start under the small overhang and pop to the bucket/rail and up.

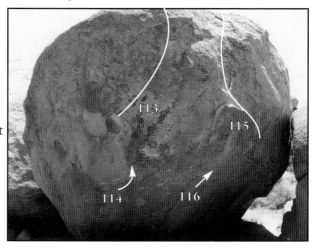

Indian Cave Boulder Map p38

117 Shindig V2 R * Surmount the slab above the cave and climb the flaring thin crack.

False Up 20 Boulder Map p38

118 False Up 20 .9 ** A tall, clean lieback flake on a vertical wall.

119 Splatterproof V0 Climb a tall knobby slab, just to the left of the descent crack.

120 Descent Crack .7 ** A clean, wide crack on a low angle face.

JBMFP Boulder (GPS = N34° 00.914 W116° 09.975) Map p38

**121 True Grit V3/4 ** Start at the corner and power the sloping arête, then lean onto the left slab.

122 JBMFP(John Bachar Memorial Face Problem) V5 ** A Josh classic. Climb the center of the vertical face on a variety of painful little holds, finishes with a big move to an incut top. Killer granite!

**123 Razarium V5 ** Slice and dice your way up razor sidepulls to join JBMFP at the top.

124 Two Stroke V3 * Jump to slopers, then dyno for the top.

125 Lechlinski Corner V3 ** Start on the left of the clean, overhanging arête, move onto the right side, then mantel over.

126 Hensel Face V2 Climb left and up across the blank slab.

127 Penny Pincher V0- Climbs a smooth slab with edges.

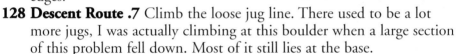

128 Descent Route .7 Climb the loose jug line. There used to be a lot more jugs, I was actually climbing at this boulder when a large section of this problem fell down. Most of it still lies at the base.

129 Death Series V1 Mantel, plain and simple.

130 Browning Arête V4 A blunt, slabby arête with grainy friction.

131 Slick Willie V2 * A friction slab, moving up and right over a small roof.

132 Skip's Arête V6 A blunt, grainy arete with relentless, gut wrenching sloper.

133 The Terminator V5 Tedious bulge moves onto a slab.

134 English Leather V1 Slabby crimps with bad feet.

Photo: R. Miramontes

Brandi Proffitt Mulligan
on White Rastafarian

Chapter 5

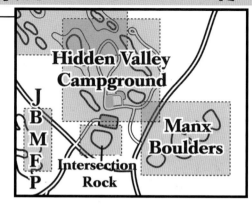

Intersection Rock

This formation is ground zero for all of the rock climbing in Joshua Tree. Several problems lie at the base of Intersection Rock. Check out the cool Intersection Traverse, and try to figure out Mediterranean Sundance, legend has it that some tall guy did it once (non run-n-jump), most deem it impossible. From the West Entrance, travel 8.8 miles to the intersection, turn left, and park in the large parking lot. Intersection Rock is the large, free standing formation on the right. Map p18, 46

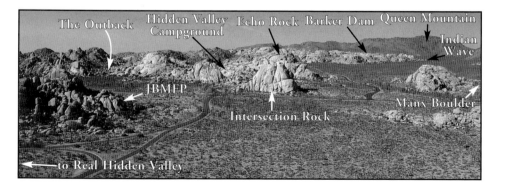

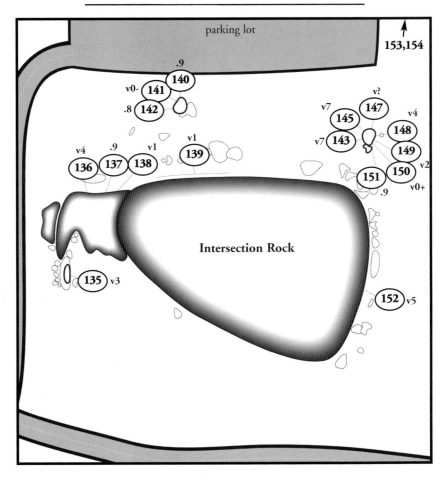

135 The Punk V3

136 Reider Problem V4 **

137 Knuckle Cracker .9 *

138 Augie Problem V1 *

139 Intersection Traverse V1 ***

140 Split End Left .9

141 Split End Right V0-

142 Fling .8

143 Anglosaxophone V7 *

144 Anglosaxophone(no cheatstone V9) *

145 Sweetspot V7 *

146 Mediterranean Sundance
(run-n-jump) V7 *

147 Mediterranean Sundance ???

148 Intersection Boulder Right V4

149 Intersection Boulder Center V2 **

150 Intersection Boulder Left V0+ *

151 Intersection Mantel .9

152 Moon Lieback V5

153 Unnamed .7

154 Pothole Problem V0

Punk Boulder This boulder is located on the western tip of Intersection Rock. Map p46

135 The Punk V3 A short, flaring crack/groove over a bulge on grainy rock. Funky landing.

Intersection Wall The right side of the north face. Map p46

136 The Reider Problem V4 **
Slabby edging over a small bulge.

137 Knuckle Cracker .9 *
A 20 ft. low angle crack widening towards the top and then finishing with nice jams.

138 Augie Problem V1 *
Up the ramp to the left arête, then up dishes. Move into the crack at the top.

139 Intersection Traverse V1 ***
A killer undercling flake that traverses about 40 feet, from left to right.

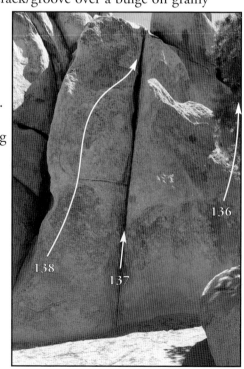

SPLIT END ROCK Located 30 ft. in front of Intersection Wall. Map p46

140 Split End Left .9 Start at a high dish and pull over the grainy face.

141 Split End Right V0- Start at the dish, traverse the horizontal crack, then over a grainy bulge.

142 Fling .8 Start at slopers and pull over double bulges.

INTERSECTION BOULDER (GPS = N34° 00.903 W116° 09.765) Located on the right side of the North Face. Map p46

143 Anglosaxophone V7 * Start on a large cheatstone, then surmount a bulging slab with terrible, sloping crimps.

144 Anglosaxophone (no cheatstone) V9 * A more esthetic start to this desperate friction problem.

145 Sweet Spot V7 * Heinous lieback maneuvers on a low angle sloping

seam and a blunt arete.

146 Mediterranean Sundance (run and jump) V7 * Bank off of the scooped out face and stick to small slopers.

147 Mediterranean Sundance ??? Stem up the concave, overhanging face to slopers above.

148 Intersection Boulder Right V4 Climbs a desperate slab, behind a bush.

149 Intersection Boulder Center V2 ** Climb the center of the slab on slopers and friction.

150 Intersection Boulder Left V0+ Climbs a slab with plates and such.

151 Intersection Mantel .9 A short mantel problem.

MOON LIEBACK Located on the east face of intersection rock. Map p46

152 Moon Lieback V5 Build a cheater to start this desperate lieback over a bulge with desperate feet.

LOOP ROCK (GPS = N34° 00.980 W116° 09.727) Located 100ft. from NE corner of the Intersection parking lot. Map p46

153 Unnamed .7 * Climbs a sharp arete/dihedral with a flaring crack to slopers.

154 Pothole Problem V0 Climb solution pockets with funky sloper moves.

Photo: R.Miramontes

Dan Mills on Dark Matter

Chapter 6

Hidden Valley Campground

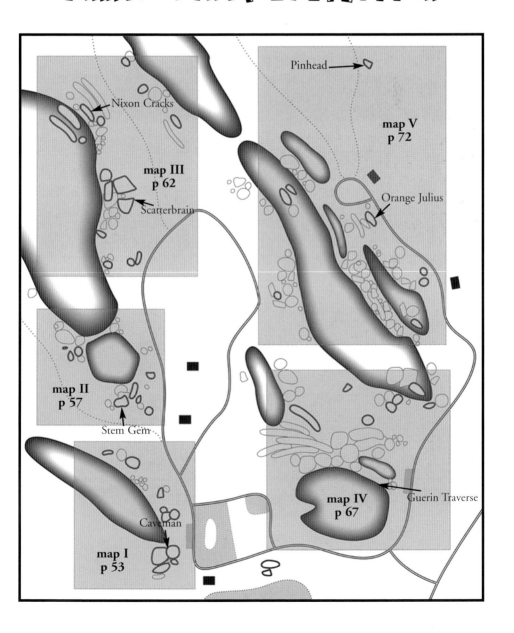

Pinhead

Nixon Cracks

**map III
p 62**

Scatterbrain

**map V
p 72**

Orange Julius

**map II
p 57**

Stem Gem

**map I
p 53**

Caveman

**map IV
p 67**

Guerin Traverse

Hidden Valley Campground

The most popular circuit in the park, with a high concentration of problems in and around the campsites. Classics in this area include Caveman, Stem Gem, Scatterbrain and Orange Julius. From the West Entrance, travel 8.8 miles to the first intersection, turn left and park in the Intersection parking lot. Parking also exists in the campground loop. Ask permission for problems in occupied sites. Maps p18, 51

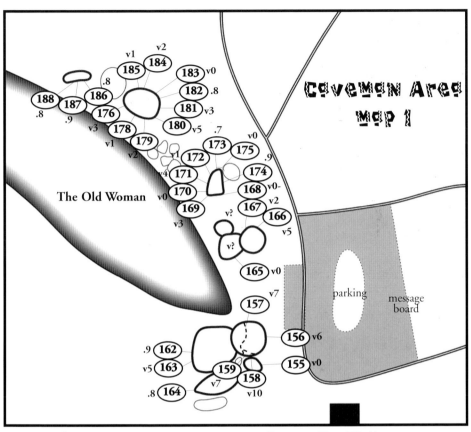

Caveman Area Map 1

The Old Woman

parking   message board

155 Brief Squeeze V0
156 Cashbox V6
157 Caveman V7 ****
158 Caveman (sit) V10 **
159 The Missing Link V7 *
160 Full Missing Link V9 **
161 Monkeyclaw V10 ***
162 Bushwack .9
163 Unnamed V5
164 Split Grain .8
165 Press Test V0
166 Basketball Jump V5
167 Roundup V2
168 Triangle Boulder South Face V0-
169 Century Bell V3
170 Old Triangle Classic V0 *
171 Triangle Face Center V4

172 Dynamo Hum V1 **
173 Descent Route .7
174 East Face Direct .9
175 Easter Bunny Back Scratcher V0
176 Mumbles Mumblephone V4 **
177 Mumbles (sit) V6 *
178 Mantel of Authority V1
179 Mantel of the New Adonis V2
180 Largonaut V5
181 Cheesegrater V3
182 N. Face Left .8
183 N. Face Center V0
184 Varsity Crank V2
185 Jr. Varsity Mantel V1
186 Snack .8
187 Morsel .9
188 Tidbit .8

Caveman Boulder

(GPS = N34° 00.975 W116° 09.795) Map p53

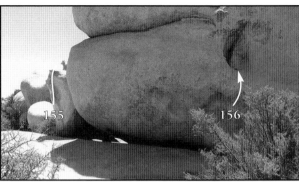

155 Brief Squeeze V0 A short overhung face starting off a terrible pinch with bad feet to not so good holds, sandbag.

156 Cashbox V6 Run and jump to the obvious large hueco/dish.

157 Caveman V7 **** Start off of the right boulder and grab a high plate on the right side of the cave, traverse the 25 foot roof on incredible buckets, dishes, fins, and huecos. Finish on the highest bucket or farthest left bucket. V8 if you avoid the "hidden" hueco in the chimney. V8 if you climb it from left to right.

158 Caveman (sit start) V10 ** Sit start at a right hand pinch, left hand undercling, and power the severely overhanging "belly" of rock, up to the starting plate of Caveman. Finish Caveman for 30+ feet of pumpy roof climbing.

159 The Missing Link V7 * Start at the Caveman plate, then move right on slopers to a lone crimp, and a long cross move right over a back grinding rock.

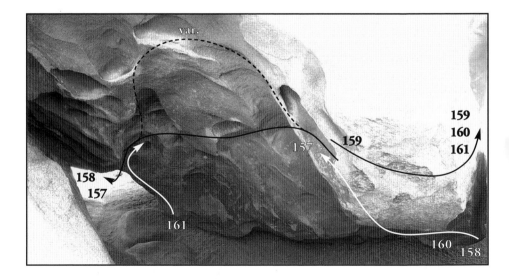

160 Full Missing Link V9 **
Sit start same as Caveman
Sit, punch straight out to the
big plate and finish the
Unnamed.

161 Monkeyclaw V10 ***
Sit start at the low point of
the cave on the left, right
hand at a low hueco, left at a
long sloper. Move straight
into the crux of Caveman,
reverse Caveman, then finish
Missing Link.

162 Bushwack .9
A short grainy jam crack.

163 Unknown V5
Gritty edges up to slopers.

164 Split Grain .8
A short gritty lieback arete.

165 Press Test V0 Hop to a
juggy dish and mantel.

166 Basketball Jump V5
Run-n-jump the bulging face
to a high jug.

167 Round Up V2 Jump to a
dish and mantel.

Triangle Boulder (GPS =
N34° 01.008 W116° 09.807) Map p53

**168 Triangle Boulder South
Face V0-** Climb to a large
flat edge left of the blunt
arête, mantel onto the big
edge and pull onto the ramp
above.

169 Century Bell V3 Lieback
the blunt arête to a jug.

170 Old Triangle Classic V0 *
Start at an incut edge and
climb slick edges and smears
on a slab.

171 Triangle Face Center V4 Greazzy edges and smears up the center of the steep slab finishing left.

172 Dynamo Hum V1 ** Start at an incut sidepull, climb up and right on crimps and buckets. Vertical to slightly overhanging.

173 Descent Route .7

174 East Face Direct .9

175 Easter Bunny Back Scrapper V0 Hook from left to right along a low shelf, then mantel and climb the upper arête.

School Boulder Map p53

176 Mumbles Mumblephone V4 ** Start low on the arête, traverse right on thin holds and technical feet up to small slopers.

177 Mumbles (sit) V6

178 Mantel of Authority V1 Mantel on the left rail.

179 Mantel of the New Adonis V2 Mantel on the right rail/sloper.

180 Largonaut V5 Campus along a gritty flake on a bulging blunt arête, turn onto the slab.

181 Cheesegrater V3 A steep slab problem wih sloping crimps.

182 N. Face Left .8 A tall friction slab.

183 N. Face Center V0- climbs a 18 ft. tall slab up angling over a bush.

184 Varsity Crank V2 A short crimp problem.

185 Jr. Varsity Mantel V2 A short mantel problem.

Snack Boulder

Located behind Mumbles. Map p53

186 Snack .8

187 Morsel .9

188 Tidbit .8

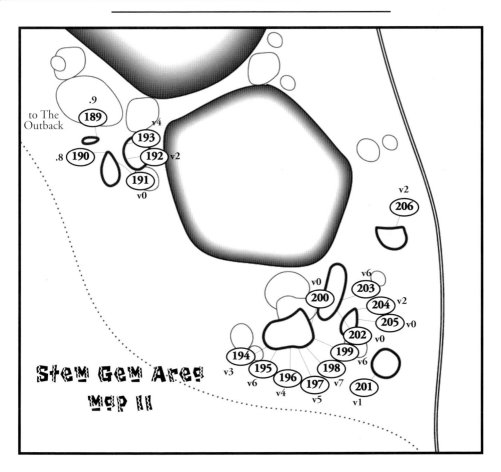

189 Nessy .9
190 Triangle Two Arete .8 R
191 Slider V0
192 Black Pea V2
193 Nugget V4
194 Slam Dunk V3 *
195 Air Johnson V6 *
196 Stem Gem V4 *****
197 Stem Gem Mantel V5

198 Vicegrip V7
199 Realized Ultimate Reality Lieback V6
200 The Piss Crack V0*
201 Sloperfest V1
202 Lemming V0
203 Yabolator V6 **
204 The Totem V2
205 Pusher V0
206 Boondogle V2

Triangle Two Boulders (GPS = N34° 01.066 W116° 09.855) This boulder can be found by walking past Stem Gem 100 yds, around the front of the formation. Map p57

189 Nessy .9 Lieback the left side, then go right around the beak and over.

190 Triangle Two Arête .8 R Mantel up from the overhanging side of the grainy arête, move left higher up. Bad landing.

191 Slider V0 Friction and edge up the center of the face.

192 Black Pea V2 Edges, up and left to gold knobs on a slab.

193 Nugget V4

Stem Gem Boulder(GPS = N34° 01.032 W116° 09.821) Map p57

194 Slam Dunk V3 * Jump off of a nearby boulder and slam the big, sloping hueco. An equally challenging mantel follows. Try not to get dunked!

195 Air Johnson V6 * Run up Stem Gem, angling left to a dish. Finish up the water groove.

196 Stem Gem V4 ***** The quintessential Joshua Tree boulder problem! Stem up the featureless concave face, traversing right to a large bump, then up the flaring groove/crack.

197 Stem Gem Mantel V5 Mantel onto the big slope, then finish up the flare.

198 Vice Grip V7 Start at the big slope, fire right to a angled rail/seam, then finish up the flare.

199 Realized Ultimate Reality Lieback V6 A short, pinned, hairline crack in a slab over a low bulge.

200 The Piss Crack V0 * An overhanging hand crack with stemming, tall.

201 Sloperfest V1 A burly little sloper problem up large, faint hueco's

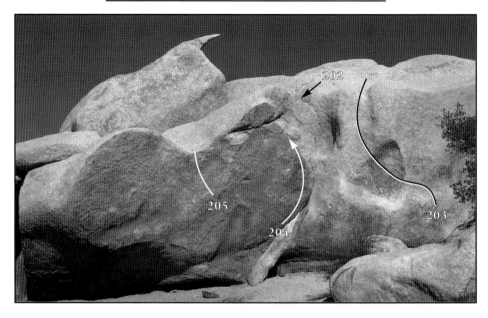

202 The Lemming V0- Leap from one boulder to a dish on the Yabolator Boulder, then mantel it out.

203 Yabolator V6 ** Start between two large, faint dishes, mantel into the left dish and traverse left to high slopers.

204 The Totem V2 Start at a low diagonal rail and send the cruxy little arete with small crimps.

205 Pusher V0

206 Boondogle V2 Start at a high jug and pull over onto the slab.

Scatterbrain Area

207 Tex Mex V1 A short thin crack in smooth granite.
208 Pitfall .9 R * A 18 ft. high clean, brown patina face with sweet edges. Rocky landing.

Hensel Boulder Map p62
209 Northeast Arete .9 Friction problem.
210 Slap Prow V3 Power over the right side of the short arete.
211 Carved Scoop .6 Climb suspect dishes on a slab.
212 Hensel Face V0 Pure friction up a 12 ft. slab
213 Slabmaster V3 Pure friction problem.
214 Hensel Arête V0+ * Friction up a slabby buttress/arête.
215 Pocket Change V1 * Start at a sloper hoeco and fire to a jug.
216 Scoop Problem V2 * Bizarre moves out a roof bowl with a low slab.

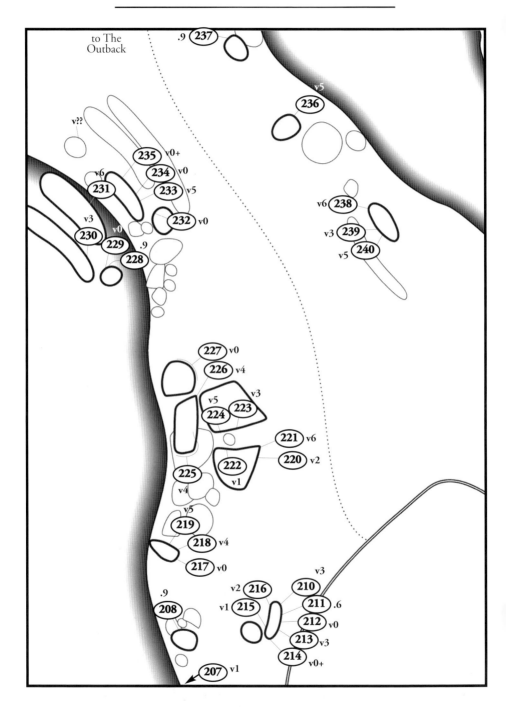

to The
Outback

.9 237

v5
236

v??

235 v0+

234 v0

v6
231

233 v5

v6 238

232 v0

v3 239

v3
230

v0
229

v5 240

228

.9

227 v0

226 v4

v5 v3

224 223

221 v6

222

220 v2

225

v1

v4

v5

219

218 v4

217 v0

v3
210

v2 216

.9

v1 215

211 .6

208

212 v0

213 v3

214 v0+

207 v1

Scatterbrain Area Map III

The Roasted Peanut Map p62

217 Ceaders Slab V0 Climb a plated slab above a small roof , angling left higher up. Poor rock on upper slab.

218 Midwest Madness V4 Start on low edges on a grid-like patina face straight up to a big plate. Traverse left across upper slab (rotten rock).

219 The Roasted Peanut V5 Start low on a diagonal, flaring seam. Traverse left along the grainy seam to edges, continue left across the plated slab.

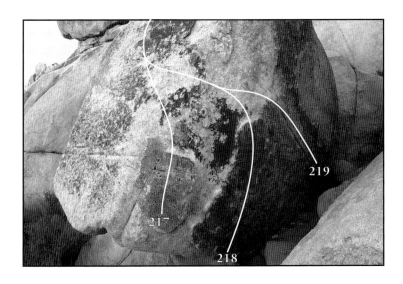

Scatterbrain Boulder (GPS = N34° 01.112 W116° 09.810) Map p62

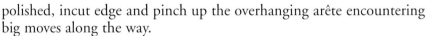

220 Bards Ankle V2 * Starts with a funky lieback flake, onto a slab with a delicate finish.

221 Scatterbrain V6 ***
Start at a polished, incut edge and pinch up the overhanging arête encountering big moves along the way.

222 Lapse of Logic V1 * Start at a sloping ledge and climb straight up, or left (slightly harder) to a sloper.

Function Boulder Map p62

223 The Function V3 R/X ***
Step off of a boulder to a small, curved shelf on a 25 ft. tall slab. Cruxy intro moves lead to edges high off the deck. Bad landing.

224 Crazy Brit Problem V5 X * Step off a boulder to acess a small curved shelf, traverse left and up on dicey thin edges and smears. Bad landing.

225 Bachar's Traverse V4 **

226 Formula One V4 Campus slopers to a big edge and an arête. Traverse into the chimney and downclimb.

227 Granite Slab V0 Friction and edge right, above the lip of a low roof on Yosemite-like granite.

228 Slab 1 .9
Short friction problem.

229 Slab B V0 Short friction problem.

230 Unwanted Crack V3 Sit start and climb an overhanging lieback crack.

231 Central Scrutinizer V6 R * A short overhanging, flaring tips crack. Potential to fall of a small cliff.

232 Hostess V0 A short slab problem.

NIXON CRACKS (GPS = N 34 ° 01.151 W116° 09.852) Walk past The Function about 100 yds., look for the wall tucked behind rocks, on the left. Map p62

233 Watergate Scandal V5 R * Walk up onto a big flake on a steep slab, reach far left for a seam with a fin, lay it off and prepare for a desperate sloper finish.

234 Left Nixon Crack V0 R *** Climbs a beautiful hand/ off hands crack on a vertical face with a small overhang at the top.

235 Right Nixon Crack V0+ R ** A nice tips crack leads to a wide slot, then sweet jams to the top of a vert. Face.

Mystic Vibrations (GPS = N34°
01.179 W116° 09.833) Located across the
small canyon from the Nixon Cracks,
on the backside of a round boulder.
Map p62

236 Mystical Vibrations V5 *
Sit start under the roof on a killer
hueco, chuck to a big shelf, then
power over the rounded arête.
Slightly grainy.

237 Patina Rail .9 *
Sweet patina plates on a slightly less
than vertical face.

Grit Rock (GPS = N34° 01.154 W116°
09.803) Located 50 yds past The
Function on the right. Map p62

238 Breathless V5
Sit start at a large jug under the low
roof and a sloper higher up, climb the pointy arete on coarse rock.

239 The Palmist V3 * Stem up the shallow, concave face to a tricky mantel

240 Feel the Grit V5 Start at double pinches over a bush and pull the sloper top.

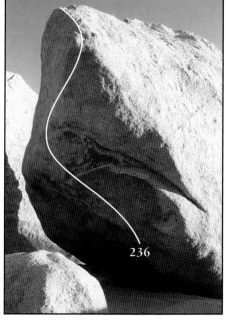

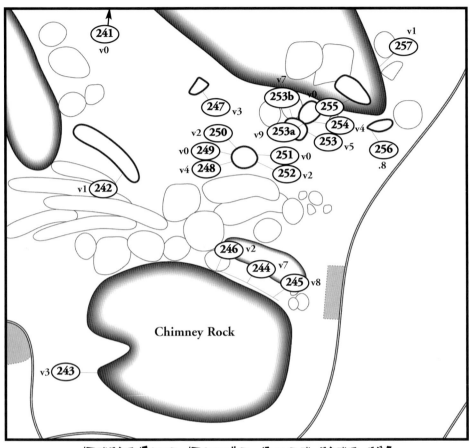

Campfire Circle Area Map IV

241 The Blank V0 R
242 Lunal Lieback V1 *
243 Copper Penny V3 R **
244 Guerin Traverse V7 *
245 Guerin Full Reverse V8 *
246 Rats with Wings V2 R **
247 Crack of Noon V3
248 Crystal Arete V4
249 Campfire Circle Mantel V0
250 Weenie Roast V2 **

251 Weenie Arete V0
252 Weenie Undercling V2
253 The Pisser V5
253a Bittersweet V9 **
253b Unnamed V7 R/X **
254 Razor Burn V4 *
255 Last Tango in JT V0
256 Phallus .8 R
257 Upsidedown Pineapple V1 *

Blank Boulder Map p67

241 The Blank V0 R Climb off a high
boulder onto a slab with a shallow crack.

Lunar Corridor (GPS = N34° 01.030 W116° 09.709) Map p67

242 Lunar Lieback V1 * A 14 ft.
vertical lieback crack tucked in a small
corridor.

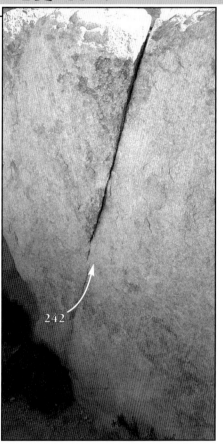

Chimney Rock (GPS = N34° 01.001 W116° 09.702) Map p67

243 Copper Penny V3 R *
Climb a small ramp up to a
roof/hueco, exit the roof/hueco
right, to a sloping hueco 20 ft.
up, finish up a low angle
pocketed seam. *Caution;* the
chimney downclimb has
unstable blocks due to recent
massive rockfall, an RV sized
block that used to house the
lead climb Loose Lips
dislodged from the roof several
years ago, filling the chimney
with loose block.

Guerin Corridor Map p67

244 Guerin Traverse V7 This old aid route is now climbable thanks to scarring. Traverses 25 ft. from left to right pulling horizontal seams on vertical terrain with technical climbing. Starting at a short finger crack and finishing at Rats with Wings.

245 Guerin Full Reverse V8 * Start at Rats with Wings, traverse left on the horizontal seams of Guerin Traverse, continuing past the thin crack on slopers and eventually pulling onto the ledge. 35 ft. traverse.

246 Rats with Wings V2 R ** An awkward thin crack leads to sweet overhanging jams high up.

Boulder of Noon (GPS = N34° 01.036 W116° 09.667)

50 yds. past Campfire Boulder, keeping to the right. Map p67

247 Crack of Noon V3 A thuggy little shallow, thin crack on a vertical face.

Campfire Circle Boulder Walk past the campsite and walk down the wash for 50 yds. Map p67

248 Crystal Arete V4 Sit start and climb a short, overhanging crystal dike arête. This problem is viscously sharp.

249 Campfire Circle Mantel V0 Jump to the ledge and mantel.

250 Weenie Roast V2 ** Climb out a small roof with funky moves to slopers.

251 Weenie Arete V0+ Start at a low sidepull and a high sloper, go left to a long rail, then up.

252 Weenie Undercling V2 High edges and an undercling to slopes.

Campsite Grotto
(GPS = N34° 01.027 W116° 09.638) Map p67

253 The Pisser V5 * A flaring seam with a pin scar, above a roof , finishing up and right on friction.

**253a Bittersweet V9 ** Start on a low horizontal rail, climb rails and crimps up and left to slopers, joining The Pisser at the top.

**253b Unnamed V7 R/X ** Start low and climb the 20 ft. tall vertical face on thin plates. Bad landing.

254 Razorburn V5 Micro crimps on a less than vertical wall.

255 Last Tango in JT V0 An awkward mantel into a bowl with an easy exit crack 20 ft. up.

256 Phallus .8 Climb the left arête of a giant flake sticking 20 ft. into the air. Downclimb or jump to a nearby slab.

257 Upside Down Pineapple V1 * Traverse right on a clean finger crack in the corner under a small roof.

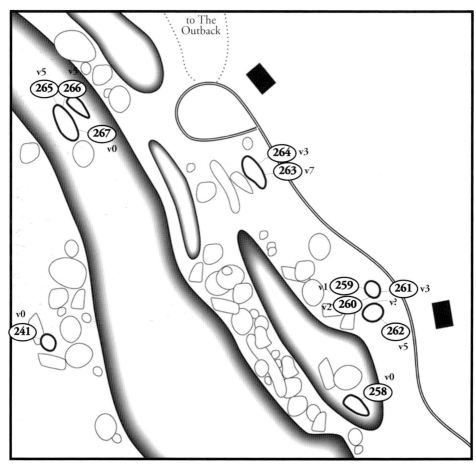

Orange Julius Area Map 5

258 Are We Having Fun Yet V0 R
259 Hershey Kiss W. Arete V1
260 Hershey Kiss S. Arete V2
261 Hershey Kiss E. Arete V3
262 Firee or Retiree V5

263 Orange Julius V7 ****
264 Lemon V3 *
265 Double Orifice V5 *
266 Double Orifice Direct V5 **
267 Hoofer V0

258 Are We Having Fun Yet V4

Hershey Kiss (GPS = N34° 01.089 W116° 09.620) Map p72
259 Hershey Kiss W. Arete V1 Sit start at a big undercling, climb up to an arête angling right to the pointy top. Grainy rock.
260 Hershey Kiss S. Arete V2 Lieback the fin-like arête , past a suspect hold, angling left to the pointy top.
261 Hershey Kiss E. Arete V3 Power a short, bulging arête on crumbly rock.
262 Fir'e or Retire'e V5 Extreme friction up a steep slab with enticing little black knobs.

Orange Julius Boulder (GPS = N34° 01.128 W116° 09.652) Map p72

263 Orange Julius V7 *** Start at shallow undercling hueco's and yard out the bulge along a brilliant orange dike with widely spaced mini-jugs and no feet. Notoriously height dependant.

264 Lemon V3 Awkward moves up a concave face to a sloping groove. Tricky!

Orifice Boulder (GPS = N34° 01.138 W116° 09.727) Map p72

265 Double Orifice V5 * Sit start under the roof on a jug, climb right through sloping huecos, to cheesegrater slopers on a slab, up to little gold knobs.

266 Double Orifice Direct V5- ** Sit start under the roof on a jug, move left through the large hueco, then up to a black knob. Join the other problem at the top.

267 Hoofer V0 knobby slab.

Chapter

7

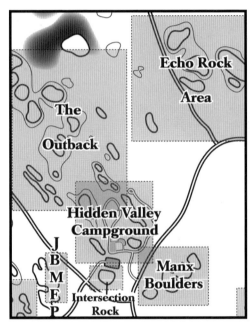

Echo Rock
Area

The
Outback

Hidden Valley
Campground

J
B
M
E
P

Intersection
Rock

Manx
Boulders

This area has a variety of interesting problems from splitter offwidths - Hobbit Hole O.W., classic highballs - White Rastafarian, to roof climbing - Scorpion Traverse. This area is accessed either from the campground or Echo Rock parking lot. Map p18

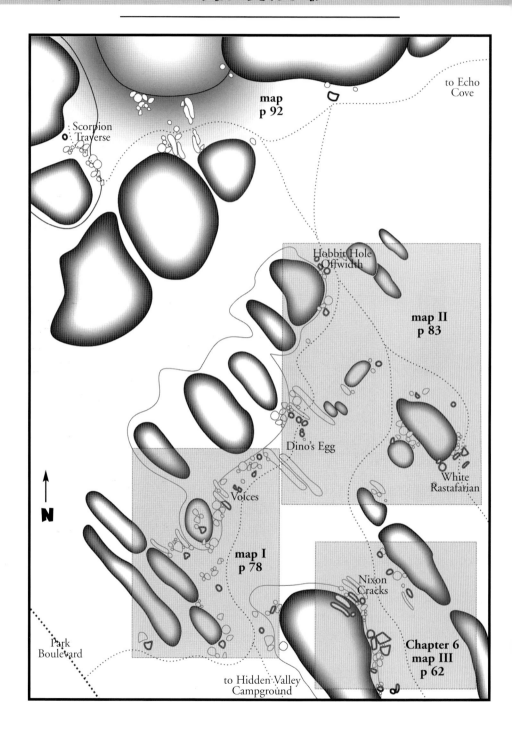

to Echo
Cove

map
p 92

Scorpion
Traverse

Hobbit Hole
Offwidth

map II
p 83

Dino's Egg

White
Rastafarian

Voices

N

map I
p 78

Nixon
Cracks

Park
Boulevard

Chapter 6
map III
p 62

to Hidden Valley
Campground

Dike Boulder (GPS = N34° 01.113 W116° 09.939) Located right on the tip of the Sidewinder formation. Map p78

268 Poor Man's Sidewinder V2 *
Start at a pointy knob, mantel up and walk along the sculpted dike. Almost a exciting as the route.

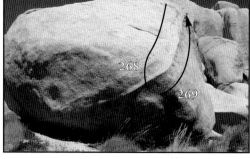

269 Gripped and Grunged V4 **
Start at a pointy knob and hand traverse the sculpted dike to a bucket.

270 Laura Scudder V2 Climb a sculpted, overhanging arête with pinches and sidepulls. Traverse right to hollow sounding plates and gently pull over.

False Hueco Boulder (GPS = N34° 01.054 W116° 09.932) Walk down the wash, into the canyon. False Hueco lies just past Laura Scudder on the right, up on a platform. Map p78

271 Torquemeister V4- Sit start at a low rail and pimp tiny knobs over a small bulge and onto a short slab.

272 Unnamed V4 * Sit start at False Hueco, go left on a horizontal rail and finish at Torquemeister.

273 False Hueco V1 **** Sit to start this short, steep overhang with incut rails and sloping huecos to buckets. Nice stone.

274 The Anti-Hueco V5 Start False Hueco, but climb the right side of the upper hueco.

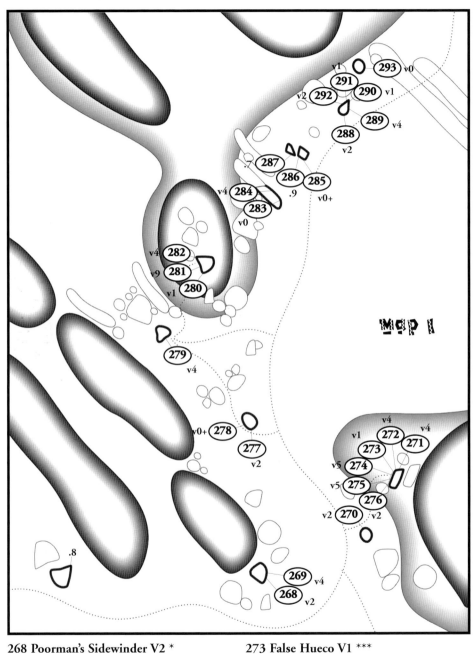

Map 1

268 Poorman's Sidewinder V2 *
269 Gripped and Grunged V4 **
270 Laura Scudder V2
271 Torquemeister V4-
272 Unnamed V4 *

273 False Hueco V1 ***
274 The Anti Hueco V5
275 Black Streak Dyno V5 **
276 False Hueco Traverse V2 *
277 Cole Arete V2 *

275 Black Streak Dyno
V5 ** Start False Hueco, traverse the rail to a big sidepull, then fire up the black streak to jugs.

276 False Hueco
Traverse V2 * Start False Hueco, then traverse the rail along the lip of a low roof.

Cole Boulder This
boulder sits in the wash 100 ft. past Laura Scudder. Map p78

277 Cole Arete V2 *
A blunt arête with black fins and loose rock up high.

278 Cole Dihedral
V0+ ** Stem a clean friction dihedral. A tree is slowly taking over this problem.

279 Yabba Dabba
Don't V4 **

Start at a bucket on a diagonal crack. Chuck big, or do a committing lock to a large, black jug.

Lizzy Boulder (GPS = N34° 01.189 W116° 09.963) Walk to Yabba Dabba Don't, turn right and climb the small boulder hill. Thin Lizzy sits facing Yabba Dabba Don't, on the top of this small hill. Map p78

280 Heat Stroke V1 Sit start on the right side of a big hueco, climb along the arête and pull onto the plated slab.

281 Thin Lizzy V9 * Sit start at a small ledge, crank on small incut plates on a 40° Overhang, finishing up and right on bigger plates.

282 Not So Thin Lizzy V4 * Sit start at a big bucket, go left to the Fred Nicole crimper, then up to a bucket, topping out left.

283 Trout Chow V0- A short tips crack.

284 Unnamed V4 Start low at a large crimp, avoiding the low flake on the left for feet. Small crimps and sidepulls on a vertical face.

Voices Boulder (GPS = N34° 01.221 W116° 09.940) Map p78

285 Scissorlock V1 * A funky shallow patina crack.

**286 Voices Arete .9 ** ** Climbs a short juggy patina arête.

287 Mr. H .7 Climbd a short juggy patina face/arête.

Tilt-o-Meter Boulder Map p78

288 Bulgemaster V2 * Start at a jug and a hueco, send a small overhang with slopes, then mantel over.

289 Bushmaster V4 Start at low, incut edge, punch out left to a thin plate, then over on a sidepull flake.

290 Tilt-o-Meter Left V1 * Sit start at a low flake, move out left to a juggy crack, then up.

291 Tilt-o-Meter Center V1 * Sit at the flake, jug straight over the prow to slopers.

292 Tilt-o-Meter Right V2 * Sit at the flake, traverse right on overhanging buckets and rails.

293 Heel Hooker V0 Mantel the overhung arête/"point" on slopers.

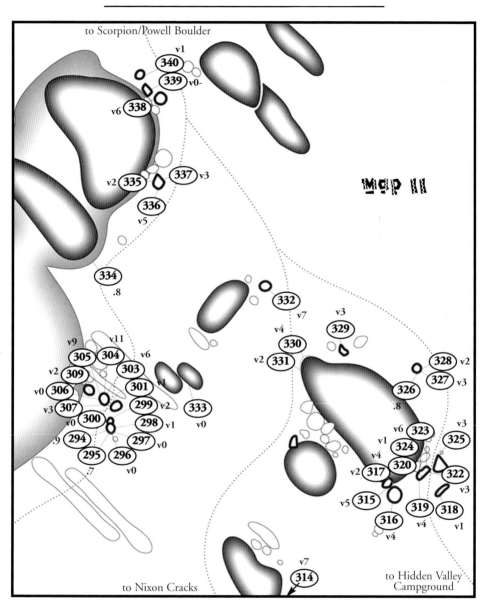

to Scorpion/Powell Boulder

v1
340
339 v0-
v6 338

v2 335 337 v3
336
v5

334
.8

332
v7
v3
329
v4
330
v2 331

Map II

v9 v11
305 304 v6
v2 309 303
v0 306 301 v1
v3 307 299 v2 333
v0 300 298 v1 v0
.9 294 297 v0
295 296
.7 v0

328 v2
327 v3
326
.8
v6 323 v3
v1 324 325
v4 320
v2 317 322
315 v3
v5 319 318
316 v4 v1
v4

to Nixon Cracks

to Hidden Valley
Campground

v7
314

331 Flake Direct V2
332 Unknown Sloper V7
333 Jug Monkey V0
334 Mr. Crack .8
335 The Mutant V2

336 Moongerms V5
337 King Smear V3 R
338 Animal V6 **
339 Hobbit Hole Offwidth V0- ***
340 Patina V1

DINO'S EGG Map p83

294 West Face .9 Patina plates and dishes on a low angle face, also the descent.

295 West Arête .7 Patina plates and edges.

296 Platypus V0 A short overhanging face up to a jug and over.

297 Dino's Egg V0 * Start up the left side of a large bowl/hueco, move out left to a sketchy top. Potential exists to fall on a large boulder.

298 The Clutch V1* Lean off of an adjacent boulder, starting low and climb sloping hueco's over a bulge.

299 Sit Down Flake V2 A silly little problem that starts sitting at small, incut flakes, and tossing for the lip of the 4 foot high boulder. Oooohh, don't fall!

Chuckawalla Boulder (GPS = N34° 01.242 W116° 09.905) Map p83
300 Flintlock Dyno V0 * Start at a big bucket and chuck for the lip of the vertical wall.
301 Chuckawalla V1 *** Climb technical sidepulls on a slightly overhung patina face.
302 Chuckawalla (sit) V6 *** Sit start at the lip of the low roof and power out right on wicked gastons, underclings, and sidepulls finishing on Chuckawalla.

Tidal Wave Boulder Map p83

303 False Tidal Wave V6 Start at sidepulls on the overhanging side of the arête, climb diagonally left and finish on the crappy left arête.

304 Tidal Wave V11 ** Start at high sidepulls and fire the sweet overhanging arête, holds have broken in recent times making this problem badass.

305 Relic V9 ** Start at Tidal Wave and traverse right on micro edges, angling up at the right end and finishing on the upper arête.

306 Bedrock Arete V0 Climb over a bulge and up a slab, climbing through a pine tree.

307 Stoney Point Problem (aka; Bambam) V3 Start on the left side of the gash pull over the round boulder.

308 Yabba Dabba Do V6 Undercling the gash right, moving out right on slopes.

Iron Door Cave Map p83

309 Iron Door Cave Problem (aka Caveman) V2 Friction, thin plates, and slopers on a slab.

Pinhead Boulder (GPS = N34° 01.200 W116° 09.700) Located 100 yds. past the campground end loop. Map p51

310 Pinhead Traverse .8 Climb the huge, jugged out dike.

311 Pinhead V1 A flaring, thin crack.

312 Paddler .8 * Friction walk up faint rails to a friction arête.

313 Holenoid V0-
  Climb over bulge and
  into a scoop.
314 Shnake V7
  A sidepull sloper hueco
  above a shelf to slopers.
315 The Jerk V5
  Start at a jug (of sorts)
  at the lip of a low roof,
  work up a short grainy
  arete, then roll over
  onto a slab.

316 Bamboozler V4 A funk-ass mantel!

317 Stiletto V2 Follow a seam up a smooth, vertical wall with edges.

318 Gizmo V1 A short little chingadera, mean as hell. Start with small
  crimps to slopers.

Family Boulder (GPS = N34° 01.236 W116° 09.724) Map p83

319 How's Your Papa V4 ** A slightly less than vertical , blunt arête with
  a big chuck for a ledge.

320 How's Your Mama V4 **** Smooth friction and sloping edges lead up
  to a shallow arch/crack with very technical moves.

321 How's your Granny V5 * Heinous slab climbing.

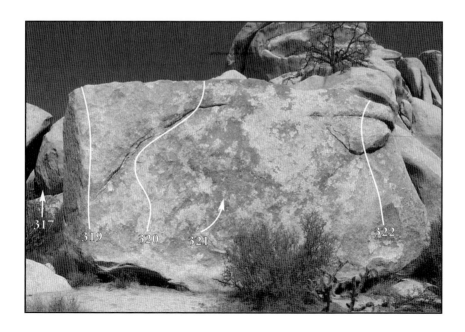

322 Little Sister V3 *Balance up onto a large footrail on a 85° face up to an undercling flake (thick).

323 Speed of Leather V6 A committing double dyno off bad underclings to ok holds. Bad landing.

324 Pigskin V1 A short overhung face.

325 White Rastafarian V3 R ***** A mega-classic, overhanging arête starting up a juggy crack and finishing with a big, fat flake.

Twin Lieback Boulder (GPS = N34° 01.303 W116° 09.762)Located behind the formation, past White Rastafarian. Map p83

326 Twin Lieback Descent .8 The easiest of three cracks.

327 Left Lieback V3 Lieback a short groove/crack up to a desperate rounded topout.

328 Right Lieback V2 Lieback a short crack to a slightly less desperate topout.

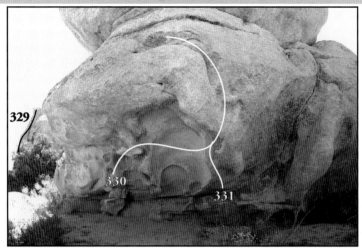

Romp Roof (GPS = N34° 01.306 W116° 09.803) Located on the west end of the formation. Map p83

**329 Blatant Disregard for Human Safety V3 R ** ** A cruxy start leads to nice jugs high off the deck.

330 Roof Romp V4 * Sit start on the left side of the roof at huecos, traverse right and out the roof to a big flake.

331 Flake Direct V2 Sit start under the right bulge and climb steep slopers straight up to a big flake.

332 Unknown Slopers V7 Start at a sidepull/sloper/dish and power up onto a desperate concave slab.

333 Jug Monkey V0 Climb a low slab up to a small roof with patina jugs.

Mr. Crack (GPS = N34° 01.309 W116° 09.895) Map p83

334 Mr. Crack .8 Clean jams on this visually uninspiring crack.

Mutant Boulder (GPS = N34° 01.354 W116° 09.855) Map p83

335 The Mutant V2 A dished out vertical face with slopers.

336 Moongerms V5 Jump to black fins and power over the bulge to a heinous seam.

337 King Smear (aka Friction Addiction) V3 * Start at the point and climb pure friction up the 20 ft. dome.

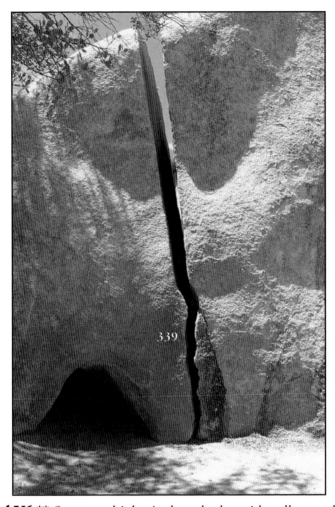

338 Animal V6 ** Start at a high pinch and a low sidepull on a short overhang, toss out left to a large pinch, then rock onto the upper left slab with balancy moves.

Hobbit Hole (GPS = N34° 01.381 W116° 09.850) Map p83

339 Hobbit Hole Offwidth V0- *** Classic O.W.! A splitter crack that goes from 4 in. to 10 in. on a smooth vertical wall.

340 Patina V1 Heinous pure friction problem.

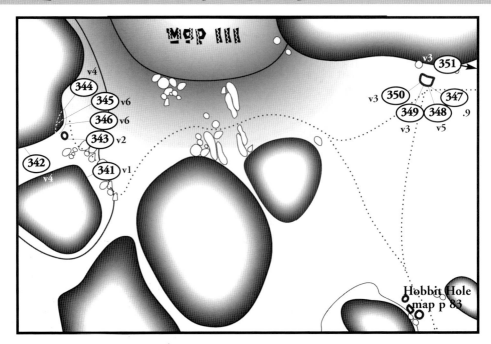

341 X Cracks V1 R
342 Digitations V4
343 Browning Slab V2
344 Scorpion Traverse V4 R **
345 Scorpion Roof Direct V6 ***
346 Viragoron Variation V6 *

347 Largotot .9
348 Largo Dyno V5 *
349 Powell Face V3 ***
350 Chollahoy V3
351 Jimmy the Weasel V3

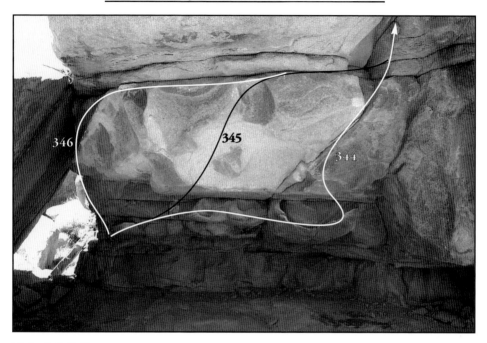

Rasta City Walk past Hobbit Hole into an open area towards a large hill with little or no rock on it. When you get to the hill turn left and walk into the canyon. Drop into a wash, angle right for 50 yds, then angle back left. This canyon should open up into a small grassy meadow, at the end of the meadow on the right is the pictured area. Map p92

341 X Cracks V1 R Knobby twin cracks with a bad landing.

342 Digitations V4 Thin cracks above a small roof with very thin holds.

343 Browning Slab V2 Climbs faint dishes on a grainy slab.

Scorpion Roof (GPS = N34° 01.473 W116° 09.059) Turn right at Rasta City and walk up the ramp/boulders (on the left side of a boulder filled gully) to a plateau area, Scorpion is tucked behind a boulder on the right side. Map p92

344 Scorpion Traverse V4 ** R Sit start at a large hueco on the left side of the roof. Follow the line of huecos out the roof to a 20 ft. tall, knobby, vertical crack. Traverse left at the top and either step off onto boulder or top out on easy patina.

345 Scorpion Roof Direct V6 * ** Sit start at the left hueco, climb straight out the roof and up to a horizontal crack with slopers. Finish up the crack.

346 Viragoron Variation V6 * Sit start at the left hueco, crimp along the left side of the roof to the horizontal crack. Traverse the crack on pumpy slopers around to the vertical crack. Finish up the crack.

Powell Boulder (GPS = N34° 01.529 W116° 09.872) The obvious lone boulder across the valley, at the base of the mountain. Map p92

347 Largotot .9 Undercling right, around, and over the giant flake. Also the downclimb.

348 Largo Dyno V5 * Start on underclings under a small roof, up to a small sloping shelf, then chuck for the top of the giant flake.

349 Powell Face V3 *** Start on the left side of the giant arching flake, move left and up to the top of the flake. Sweet granite!

350 Chollahoy V3 Climb out a short overhang to hollow flakes.

351 Jimmy the Weasel V3 A short sloper problem.

Chapter 8

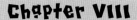

The

Lonesome West

Crowded

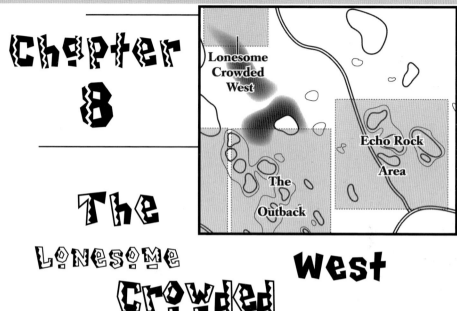

Highlights

in this area include E.J. Deluxe and the roof O.W. called Inquisition. From the West Entrance, travel 8.8 miles to the second intersection, turn left and then travel .6 mile and turn left again. From there travel approx. 1 mile to a gate with a parking area and a restroom.

The boulders are on the left as you approach the parking area. Walk towards the hillside to the obvious orange crag. This is the Rusty Wall. The boulders lie on the desert floor below this wall. Map p18,96

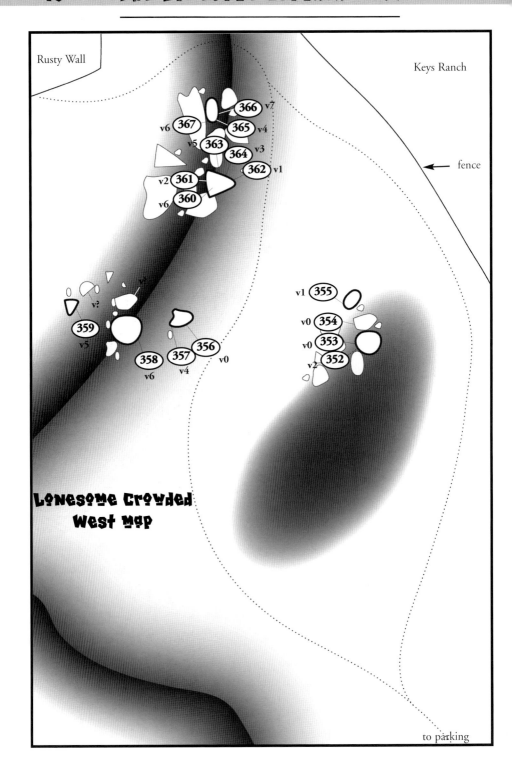

Rusty Wall

Keys Ranch

← fence

v7 366
v6 367   365 v4
v5 363
364 v3
v2 361   362 v1
v6 360

v?
359
v5

v1 355
v0 354
v0 353
v2 352

358   357   356   v0
v6   v4

Lonesome Crowded West Map

to parking

352 Custom Concern V2 Edges over a bulge.

353 Lounge V0 Thin lieback crack to jugs.

354 Shit Luck V0 Patina knobs and edges.

355 Epperson Problem V1 Wierd grey knobs high over a bulge.

All Nice On Ice

356 It's All Nice On Ice V0 Balance moves up a faint dihedral to a slopey mantel lip.

357 Doin' the Cockroach V4 ** Start low and fire slopers and an edge on a faceted arete.

INQUISITION BlQC (GPS = N34° 01.947 W116° 10.296) Map p96
358 The Inquisition V6 *** Sit start 10 ft. in the low roof, climb blocks
    and wide cracks out to a squeeze chimney and a wide crack.
359 Monster Truck Pull V5/6 * Sit start at a low jug under the roof,
    power slopers across the lip to a cruxy mantel.

JacksQNville (GPS = N34° 01.961 W116° 10.312) Map p96
360 Cumalong V6 **** Climbs a 40° overhung tips crack.
361 Trailer Trash V2 Traverse 10 ft. left on a thick flake with a crack.

362 Convenient Parking
V1 ** Climb diagonal rails up to the lower left lip of the boulder.

363 E.J. Deluxe V5 ****
Climb the center of the gorgeous 20° overhanging wall. Sit to start at the low roof and climb diagonal rails and blocks finishing just right of the apex of the boulder.

364 E.J. Deluxe Escape
V3 *** Sit start at the low roof and climb the diagonal rail escaping onto the left slab.

365 Bankrupt on Selling
V4 Start at a sidepull rail and pull the sloping lip. Bad landing.

366 Crisco Disco V7 **
Sit start matched at a jug on the corner, power right to the sidepull rail and finish Bankrupt on Selling.

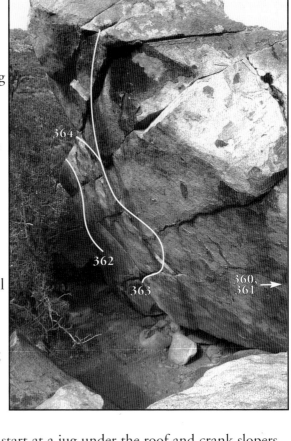

367 Cowboy Dan V6 * Sit start at a jug under the roof and crank slopers and crimps onto the slab.

Photo: R.Miramontes

Rob Guinn on Perpetual Darkness

Chapter 9

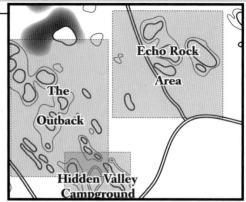

Echo Rock

The Echo Rock area is one of the most popular places for lead climbing in the park. Highlights in this area are the tall dihedral Coyote Corner, the funky stemming on the Left Peyote Crack, short steep power problems at Igneous, and the balancy Master Cylinder. From the West Entrance travel 8.8 miles to the second intersection, turn left and travel .6 mile and turn left again. Parking is abundant and restroom facilities can be found here. Map p18, 102

to Lonesome
Crowded West

Echo Cove
map
p104

Echo Rock
map
p110

v1
368

to
The
Outback

parking

parking

parking

parking

N

to Barker Dam

v3 **369**
v0 **370**
371
v3
372 **373**
.9
v3

Peyote Cracks

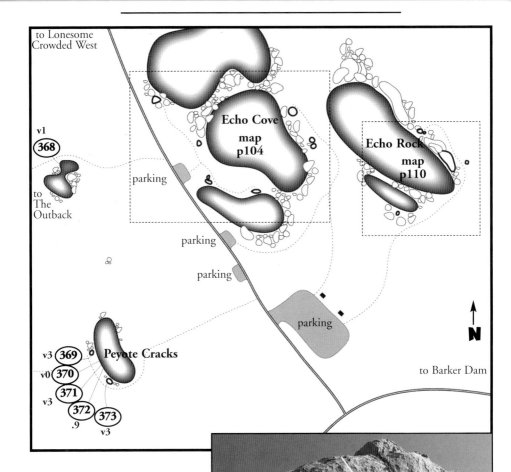

Coyote Corner (GPS = N34° 01.520 W116° 09.658) Park at the Echo Cove parking and walk 200 yds. West to a small very small formation, Coyote Corner is around the right side. Map p102

368 Coyote Corner V1 R *** Climb the smooth dihedral with a juggy crack in it. Exit right at the roof on killer patina knobs, up to rad stone. Tall!!

368

368 Coyote Corner V1 R ***
369 Grainstorm V3
370 Matt's Pinch V0+

371 Left Peyote Crack V3 **
372 Middle Peyote Crack .9 *
373 Yabble Babble V3

Peyote Cracks

This small formation sits alone in the open plains between Echo and the campground, it can be accessed from either the Echo Rock parking area or the Hidden Valley Campground. Both are about the same distance (250-300 yds). Map p102

Grainstorm Boulder Map p102
369 Grainstorm V3 A gnarly, grainy buttress.

Peyote Cracks Wall (GPS = N34° 01.340 W116° 09.646) Located on the west side of the formation. Map p102
370 Matt's Pinch V0+Bearhug the bulge up to a crack, traverse left to exit.
371 Left Peyote Crack V3 ** Awkward stems up a nice overhanging dihedral, 18 feet to a ramp/wide crack.
372 Middle Peyote Crack .9 * A clean thin crack up 16 ft. to a ramp/chimney.

Babble Boulder Map p102
373 Yabble Babble V3 Thin, painful plates and edges on slabby terrain.

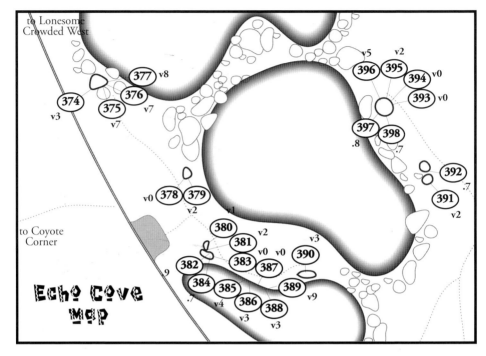

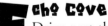
Echo Cove
Map

374 Grungy Arete V3
375 The Turtle V7 **
376 Igneous Ambiance V7 **
377 Mulligan Variation V8 **
378 Afterthought V0
379 Classic Thin Crack V2 **
380 Right Arete V1
381 Arete Boulders Face V2
382 Arete Boulders Crack .9
383 Left Arete V0+
384 Unnamed .7
385 Little Joe V4
386 Mother Tongue V3 *

387 Starter V0- *
388 Javaman V3 **
389 One Move Wonder V9
390 Kurt Smith Problem V3
391 Steam Train V2 **
392 Big Dike .7 *
393 Smear Tactics V0
394 Marginalia V0
395 Value Pack V2
396 Crimp This V5
397 Winky .8
398 Blinky .7

Echo Cove
Drive past the main parking lot and park at the third lot on the right.

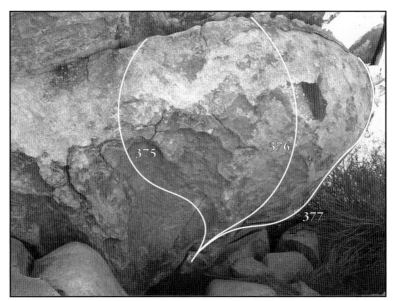

Igneous Boulder (GPS = N34° 01.556 W116° 09.558) Map p104

374 Grungy Arete V3 A blunt, grainy arête. A contender for the "worst problem in the park".

375 The Turtle V7 ** Sit start at two horns, under steep rock. Move left on incut edges and knobs (avoiding the butt dragging rock) up to plates.

376 Igneous Ambiance V7 ** Sit start at the two horns, climb the left side of the steep arête on incut edges and knobs, up to incut plates.

377 Mulligan Variation V8 ** Sit start at the two horns, climb the right side of the arête (avoiding another ass dragger).

Classic Thin Crack (GPS = N34° 01.517 W116° 09.530) Map p104

378 Afterthought V0 Climb the thin left crack to the arête.

379 Classic Thin Crack V2 ** Climbs a right leaning thin crack system on vert. Rock.

Arete Boulders
Map p104

380 Right Arête V1
A short, overhanging arête with a slopey lip.

381 Arete Boulders Face V2 Climb the left arête and crimpers on the overhanging face.

382 Arete Boulders Crack .9 A short juggy crack.

383 Left Arête V0+
Lieback the grainy, overhanging arete.

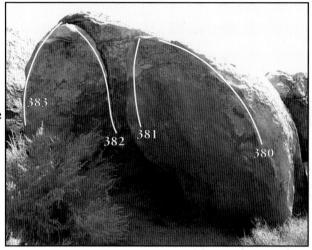

384 Unnamed .7 Climb a slabby dihedral with a crack in it.

Big Moe Wall Map p104

385 Little Joe V4 Start at a high sloping sidepull on vertical terrain angling left on funky little holds, then back right to the ramp.

386 Mother Tongue V3 * Edge or jump to a sloping tongue of rock and then power up to a rail. Traverse right to get off.

387 Starter V0- * Blocky pinches and slick jugs up to buckets.

388 Javaman V3 ** Climb a vertical wall with sidepull slopes up to buckets. Traverse right to get off.

389 One Move Wonder V9 Micro sidepulls up to a dish. Critical foothold is about to crumble.

Smith Rock
Map p104

390 Kurt Smith Problem V3
Start at a big black streak and climb a left leaning thin seam on a slab with delicate moves up to slopers.

Eᴄʜᴏ Rᴏᴄᴋ Cɪʀᴄᴜɪᴛ

From the West Entrance, travel 8.8 miles and turn at the second left. From there go .6 mile and turn left, then a quick right into a large parking area. The boulders are scattered around the formation. Map p104, 110

Big Dike (GPS = N34° 01.521 W116° 09.412)

These boulders are located in the large corridor between Echo Eock and Echo Cove, on the left side of the large wash. Map p104

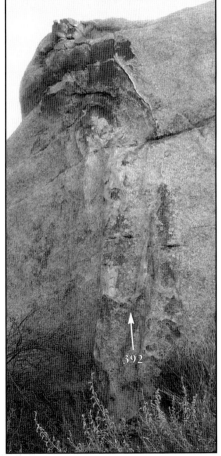

391 Steam Train V2 ** Traverse left and up along a crimpy dike feature for 20 ft. or so.

392 Big Dike .7 * Climbs an irresistible big dike.

Value Boulder Located on the left side of the wash just after the corridor opens up, 100 yds. past Big Dike. Map p104

393 Smear Tactics V0 A short slab problem.

394 Marginalia V0 A short vertical face with grainy crimps.

395 Value Pack V2 Thin, grainy crimps to an arching crack.

396 Crimp This V5 Crimp what?? Micro crimps on a short vertical face.

397 Winky .8 A short patina problem.

398 Blinky .7 A short patina problem.

Beak Rock (GPS = N34° 01.453 W116° 09.334) Located in front of Echo Rock, tucked behind a boulder that looks like a huge nose (that you can see from the parking lot). Map p110

399 Backscratcher V0- *
Climbs a crack/arête with rails, knobs, and jugs.

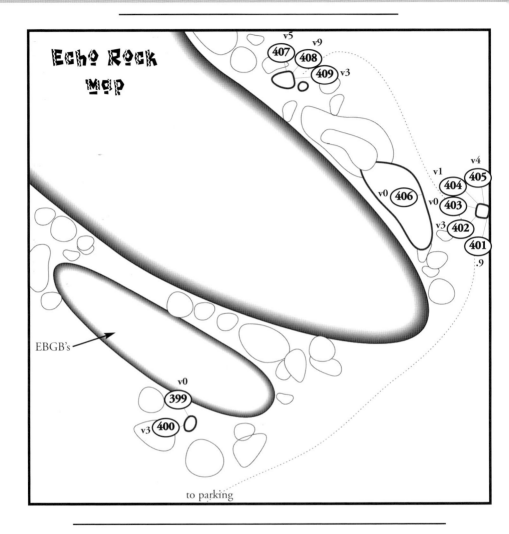

Echo Rock
Map

EBGB's

to parking

---

399 Backscratcher V0- *
400 Flake Dyno V3 *
401 Gumdrop East Corner .9
402 Gumdrop South Corner V3/4 *
403 Gumdrop West Corner V0 *
404 Northwest Face V1

405 Northeast Face V4
406 Fingerfood V0
407 Master Cylinder V5 ***
408 Don't Mess with Bill V9 **
409 Gas Guzzler V3+

400 Flake Dyno V3 *
Move left along a big plate on a gently overhanging wall, finishes with a big move to a mantel lip.

The Gumdrop (GPS = N34° 01.512 W116° 09.249) Walk around the right side of Echo Rock for approx. 400 yds. to the obvious lone boulder. Map p110

401 East Corner .9 Patina edges and plates. Also the downclimb.

402 South Corner V3/4 *
A slightly less than vertical double arête with nasty sidepulls and grainy edges. Climbs over a cactus.

403 West Corner V0 *
A textbook mantel onto the obvious shelf.

404 Northwest Face V1
Start at the arete and climb delicately onto the green lichen'y upper slab.

405 Northeast Face V4
Grainy edges and a sidepull lead to a funky legpress/mantel up to grainy slopers.

Poodle Wall This problem is on a large rock at the base of the formation, right across from The Gumdrop. Map p110

406 Fingerfood V0 * Start stemming up a concave face with a thin crack up to a juggy 25 ft. tall crack.

Patterns in the Sand (GPS = N34° 01.563 W116° 09.310) Walk around the back of Echo Rock, 150 yds. past the Poodle Wall, scrub oak trees hide this small sandy cove. Map p110

407 Master Cylinder V5 * Match start on the low rail, power up and then left on tricky slopers to the arête. Finish up the smooth, tall slab. Sandy landings.

**408 Don't Mess With Bill V9 ** Start at a high pinch at the prow of the roof. Power slopers onto the slab and up.

409 Gas Guzzler V3+ Chuck and highstep thing. Awkward, harder than it looks!

Chapter
10

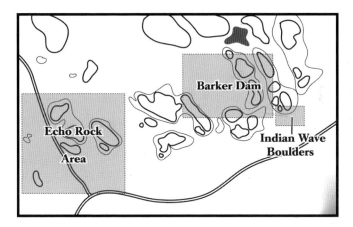

Barker Dam

Echo Rock
Area

Indian Wave
Boulders

Barker Dam

The
Barker Dam area holds some of the more unusual oddities from
Joshua Tree's many pasts. At Indian Wave, remains of a Hollywood
set, and just beyond that, a native american equinox marker. Barker Dam
itself aka; Bighorn Dam, built by miner Bill Keys in the early 1900's. Native
rock art is scattered all throught the canyons here.

Barker Dam Circuit
Highlights in this area are Gunsmoke, High Noon, Streetcar Named
Desire, and the ultra steep Diary of a Dope Fiend. From the West
Entrance, travel 8.8 miles and turn at the second left. Go 1.6 miles and turn
left into the large parking area. There are restroom facilities here.
Map p18, 119

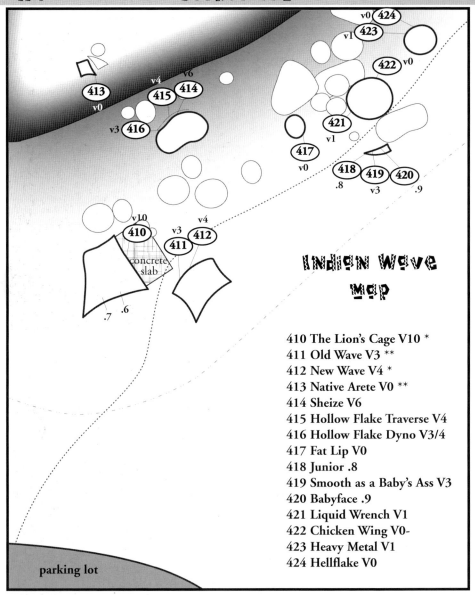

Indian Wave Map

410 The Lion's Cage V10 *
411 Old Wave V3 **
412 New Wave V4 *
413 Native Arete V0 **
414 Sheize V6
415 Hollow Flake Traverse V4
416 Hollow Flake Dyno V3/4
417 Fat Lip V0
418 Junior .8
419 Smooth as a Baby's Ass V3
420 Babyface .9
421 Liquid Wrench V1
422 Chicken Wing V0-
423 Heavy Metal V1
424 Hellflake V0

Ndian Wave Boulders

Beautiful triangular boulders comprise this small area located just beyond the parking lot. The rock here is fairly coarse.

The Lion's Cage The concrete slab and 30 ft. strip of epoxy along the boulder are courtesy of a 50's film crew, the remnants of a cage built to house lions and other animals used in the production. Map p114

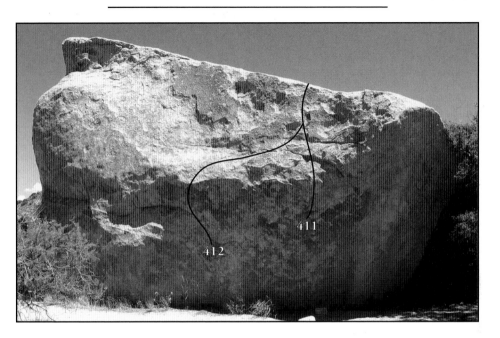

410 The Lion's Cage V10 * Start at a 8 inch long, incut, sidepull edge, move up the slightly overhanging wall on razor crimps to a long, rotten flake of patina.

Indian Wave Boulder
(GPS = N34° 01.572 W116° 08.485)
Map p114

411 Old Wave V3 **
Use a cheatstone to get to a high edge on a short overhang , up to patina plates. Downclimb tree.

412 New Wave V4 *
Start at an arching flake, climb left slightly, up onto the slab, then back right to finish same a old wave.

413 Native Arete V0 **
A beautiful knife-edge arête on unusual rock.

Sheize Roof Poor rock quality. Map p114

414 Sheize V6 Start at dishes under the roof. Power straight out the bulge on grainy slopers, onto the slab at a hollow flake/hole. Traverse right across the slab and join Hollow flake dyno. Epic!

415 Hollow Flake Traverse V4 Traverse from left to right on overhanging, grainy huecos. Finish on the hollow flake dyno.

416 Hollow Flake Dyno V3/4 Start on the big, hollow flake, fire the small overhang, then finish up the grainy crack. Downclimb the grainy crack and jump.

417 Fat Lip V0 A short arête capped by a small roof, with a nice mantel over a little cactus patch.

Shard Map p114

418 Junior .8 Climbs a clean shard of rock that cleaved off an adjacent boulder. Lieback and friction up the short arête.

419 Smooth as a Baby's Ass V3 * Clean friction 5 ft. left of Junior.

420 Babyface .9 Friction up along a diagonal dike.

421 Liquid Wrench V1 Short folk might need a cheatstone to start. Climb a right curving flake.

Equinox Marker/ Pictographs

The Indian Cave at the end of the circuit holds a fascinating relic from the past. Sitting on the floor in the center of the cave area is a stone with a large grinding hole and many smaller holes. This instrument was used by native Indians to mark the Equinox's and other specific dates. As the light first peers through the crack formed by the two boulders, it will align with the different holes on the different dates, the largest one being the Vernal Equinox.

There are also several excellent pictographs on the adjacent boulder, including the Red Woman. Several problems exist in this cave, but climbing is illegal here and rangers watch this site! Please do not climb here!

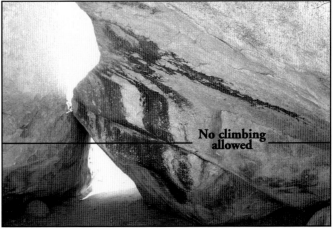

No climbing allowed

Chicken Wing (GPS = N34° 01.610 W116° 08.463) Map p114

422 Chicken Wing V0- Starts at a large, hanging plate over a roof, up to a juggy crack. Its questionable as to whether it is legal to climb this problem, as it is so close to the equinox marker.

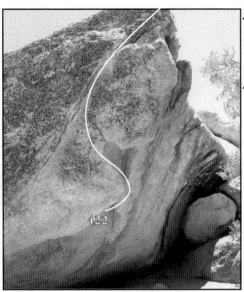

423 Heavy Metal V1 Start at double gastons at a hueco and move left and up to slopes, then jugs. Map p114

424 Hellflake V0 Start on the arête and go right up to the crack.

Barker Dam area

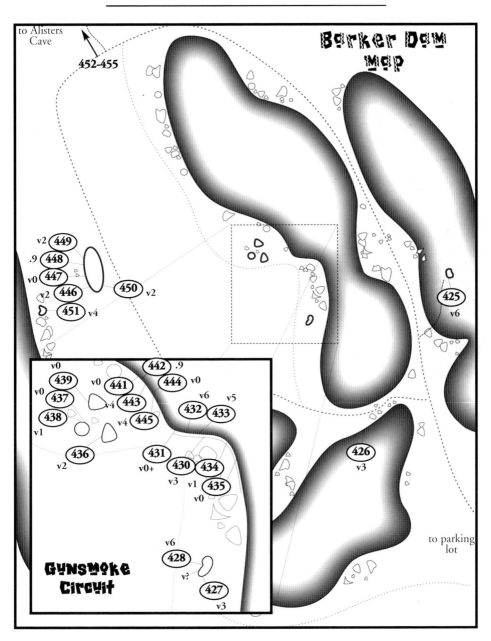

447 Retrofit V0
448 Piano Rock Crack .9
449 Black Nipples V2
450 Black Slot V2
451 Heinous Anus V4 **

452 Sex Magician V7 ***
453 Sex Magician (sit) V8
454 Perpetual Darkness V10 **
455 Diary of a Dope Fiend V8 ***

Lost Roof (GPS = N34°
01.724 W116° 08.585) Follow the
main trail from the parking
lot into the canyon, continue
straight towards Barker Dam,
when the canyon becomes
very tight (50 yds. into the
canyon), scramble up the
formation on the right,
passing nice boulders on the

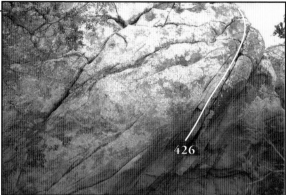

way. The Lost Roof is on the very top of the dome. Map p119

425 Lost Roof V6 Sit start at a blocky pinch. Climb left out the small roof
to rough slopes. Cruxy pulling onto the slab.

Mr. Coffee (GPS = N34° 01.586 W116° 08.670) As you enter the canyon, turn
left and go down the large trail, Mr. Coffee is hidden in the bushes on the
left just before the canyon open up to the right. Map p119

426 Mr. Coffee V3 * Climb a short, overhanging lieback crack to juggy
cracks on a slab.

Streetcar Boulder (GPS = N34° 01.659 W116° 08.694) Map p119

427 Birdman V3 A shallow groove and a dish high over a bulge.

428 Streetcar Named Desire V6/7 **** A slabby dihedral with tough stemming moves, up to a small roof and a dish over the top.

429 Streetcar (run and jump) V5 Run up the dihedral and stick the sloping dish, then mantel it out.

GUNSMOKE (GPS = N34° 01.686 W116° 08.681) Follow the main trail from the parking lot, enter the canyon and turn left, follow the trail as it turns right into a large valley, stay to the right and follow a smaller trail along the formation for 200 yds. Gunsmoke is tucked in a little alcove. Map p119

430 Gunsmoke V3 **** A 75 foot long, slightly overhanging traverse on horizontal cracks with buckets, slopers, and incut plates. Has reachy moves.

431 High Rail Left V0+ R * Traverse left up a pockety, diagonal crack. Bad yucca landing.

432 Shanghai Noon V6 ** Follows a hairline seam. Dyno from one crack to the next, then power up and right on the sloping lip, finishing in roughly the same place as High Noon.

433 High Noon V5 **** Climb overhanging, jugs to a vertical, thin crack. Finish up and left on slopers.

434 Corner Problem V1 * A slightly overhanging dihedral with crimps and flakes on bomber granite. Finishes up and right.

435 Ledge Problem V0+ Sit start and climb overhanging rails, ledges, and jugs angling slightly left.

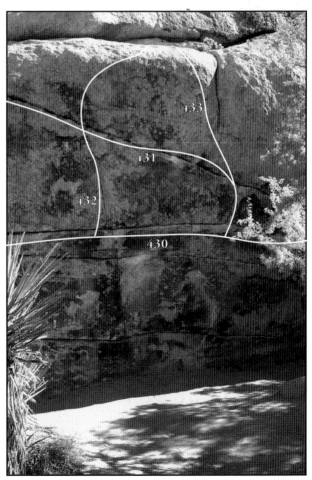

Photo: R.Miramontes

The Master of Gunsmoke

John Jenkins

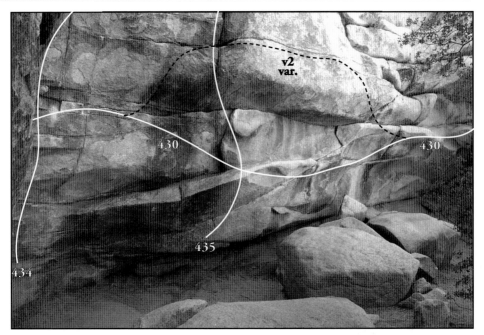

The Chube (GPS = N34° 01.705 W116° 08.718) Located 50 yds. West of Gunsmoke. Map p119

436 The Chube V2 *** A juggy diagonal crack with a big move to the sloping top. Then mantel baby, mantel.

437 Friction 100 V0- A short friction problem up the blunt arête. Also the downclimb.

438 Friction 101 V1 A short friction problem up the center of the face.

439 Unnamed V0+ Sidepulls up to jugs on a vertical wall.

440 Unnamed Variation V2 Start on low sloper and fire up to jugs.

The Chosspile

The rock here is poor quality. Map p119

441 Chosspile Direct V0 Start at a grainy flake 2 ft. right of the arête, move up to rotten jugs.

442 Stem Blem .9 The obvious crack/ corner line, loose jugs at top.

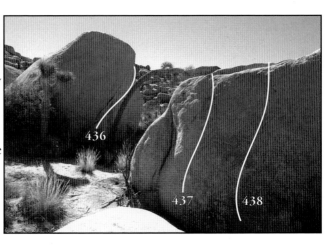

443 All Pain No Gain V4 Start low on a grainy rail and grind out the small overhang on grainy slopers.

444 Rambler V0 Sit start and climb steep jugs, traversing left, then up the lower angle face. Traverse left and downclimb.

445 Cave Girl V4 Start the same as Rambler but move straight over the bulge on slopers.

PIANO ROCK (GPS = N34° 01.683 W116° 08.874) They say cowboys used to keep a piano on top of this rock to entertain the cattle herders back in the day. The obvious large flat boulder in the middle of the canyon, 250 yds. west of Gunsmoke. Map p119

446 Balance Problem V2 A tricky little friction problem.

447 Retrofit V0 A flaring hand crack that curves right at the top.

448 Piano Rock Crack .8 A plated out finger crack. Some loose plates!

449 Black Nipples V2
Balancy moves up a
steepening slab leads to
black knobs.
450 Black Slot V2 A black
alcove/ crack to a grainy
topout.

Heinous Anus (GPS =
N34° 01.657 W116° 08.922) From
Gunsmoke, continue past

Piano Rock to the formation, Heinous Anus is in the bushes on the valley
floor. Map p119

451 Heinous Anus V4 ** Start at the obvious …hole and fire to the lip of
the overhanging face. Squeeze out a tough mantel on slopers to finish.

Alisters Cave (GPS = N34° 01.913 W116° 09.007) Continue past Gunsmoke
all the way to the North end of the valley to a very large wash. To the right
is Barker Dam, walk to the left and into the first open canyon (a bright
orange, overhanging dihedral called Clockwork Orange marks the entrance),
angle up the faint ramp on the left side of the canyon. Crawl under a notch
on the edge of a cliff (scary), continue up the now large ramp to the cave. If
you continue up the canyon floor, on the left is a cave with many
pictographs. Map p119

452 Sex Magician V7 *** A 35 ft. traverse along the edge of a huge roof.

Goes from left to right, starting at jugs, and finishing up a sketchy 22 ft. tall crack. Traverse left on upper slab to top out.

453 Sex Magician (sit) V8 ** Sit start at a grainy jug/sidepull, power out the 8 ft. roof to the regular start.

454 Perpetual Darkness V10 ** Start at a large edge and a pinch about 4 ft. high. Fire into the flaring roof crack, and power out the roof to join Diary of a Dope Fiend.

455 Diary of a Dope Fiend V8 *** Sit start at a low ledge on the far right side of the cave. Climb the 25 ft. roof with hand jams, slopers, dope plates, and did I mention slopers.

Chapter 11

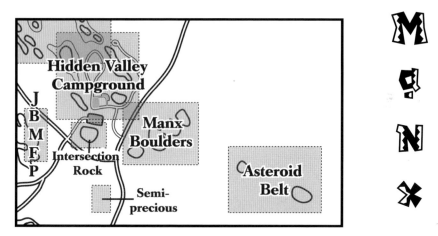

M
a
N
X

Asteroid Belt

Manx Bouldering Circuit

One of the more popular circuits in the park, due to the close proximity of the road, and the abundance of moderates in a small area. Check out the roof problems at Pigpen, and the committing Undertow. From the West Entrance, travel 8.8 miles, turn at the second left and park on the right turnout. Map p18, 128

Asteroid Belt

Must-do: Peabrain, relentless. From the West Entrance, travel 8.8 miles to the second left. Turn and park on the right. Map p18, 134

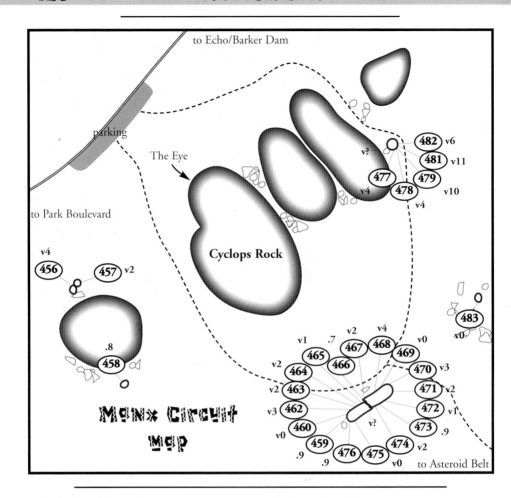

to Echo/Barker Dam

parking

The Eye

to Park Boulevard

Cyclops Rock

v? 482 v6
481 v11
477 479
478 v10
v4 v4

483
v0

v4
456
457 v2

.8
458

Minx Circuit Map

v1 .7 v2 v4
465 467 468 v0
464 466 469
v2 470 v3
463 471 v2
v2 462 472 v1
v3 460 473 .9
v0 459 474 v2
.9 476 475 v0
.9 .9
to Asteroid Belt

456 Chip flakey V4 *
457 Key Largo V2 **
458 The Womb .8
459 Right Arete .9
460 Scuttlebutt V0
461 Scuttlebutt Left Exit V4
462 Undertow V3 ***
463 The Boxer Problem V2 **
464 Xylophone V2
465 Fishbait V1
466 Unnamed .7
467 Out of Touch V2 **
468 Off Camber V4
469 Grunge V0

470 Crankcase V3
471 Wrangler V2
472 Gambit V1
473 Thingamagig .9
474 Meat Substitute V2
475 Ribtickler V0
476 South Face .9
477 Pigpen V4 ***
478 Nicopress V4 *
479 The Yogi V10 **
480 Yogi (var) V9 **
481 The Lamprect Problem V11 **
482 Struthers Problem V6
483 Unnamed V0-

Chip Flakey (GPS = N34° 00.865 W116° 09.651) Map p 128
456 Chip Flakey V4 * Cheatstone it to a very high undercling flake that curves around and back.
457 Key Largo V2 ** Climb the vert. to slabby center of the face on smooth slopes.

The Womb (GPS = N34° 00.837 W116° 09.623) Map p128

458 The Womb .8 Climb up a low angle face inside of the giagantor hueco. Make like a baby and head out the "womb" on the left side on friction.

Manx Boulders (GPS = N34° 00.860 W116° 09.497) Map p128

459 Right Arete .9 Lieback the arete.

460 Scuttlebutt V0 Friction up a concave face and surmount the bulge on awkward slopers.

461 Scuttlebutt Left Exit V4 Friction up the concave face, staying left, going over a second bulge.

462 Undertow V3 * ** Mantel onto the shelf via the thin seam , up to small slopes, over a bulge to a hueco way over the top.

463 The Boxer Problem V2 ** Thin plates on a vertical face to a large undercling, bust out slopes for the topout.

464 Xylophone V2 Small sloping edges on a vertical wall, to a rounded summit.

465 Fishbait V1 This short sloper problem starts along a diagonal rail to a faint dish.

466 Unnamed .7 Climbs a patina filled dihedral.

467 Out of Touch V2 ** Start in the face and move right into a sidepull/undercling, then right to the arête. Work up the sloper arête to a cruxy mantellip.

468 Off Camber V4 Start at a sloping shelf, toss for the lip, Mantel through the tree. If you want the send, you gotta mantel it out!!!!

469 Grunge V0 Climbs a large flake.

470 Crankcase V3 Punch up a short flaring lieback crack.

471 Wrangler V2 An awkward little mantel problem.

472 Gambit V1 Thin crimps over a small bulge.

473 Thingamagig .9 Edge up a slab to a large protruding jug system.

474 Meat Substitute V2 A sharp, grainy arete with edges on the face.

475 Ribtickler V0 Climb between two large dishes to a large ,arching, blunt flake.

476 South Face .9 A rough mantel up into a large bowl to easy climbing.

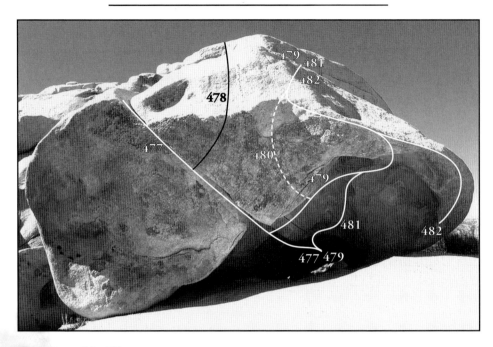

PigPeN BoulDer (GPS = N34° 00.915 W116° 09.482) Map p128

477 Pigpen (aka. Bachar Cracker of the Desert) V4 *** Sit start at the "tongue" in the roof crack (or further) , climb out the 10 ft roof via the hand and finger crack to a pumpy thin hand crack.

478 Nicopress V4 * Jump or climb crack to get to jugs at the lip of the overhang. An awkward, in your face mantel gets you over.

479 The Yogi V10 ** Climb Pigpen to the giant bucket, then move right into the bowl/roof with contortionistic moves, finish same as the Lamprect Problem.

480 The Yogi (variation finish) V9 ** After the rest, move into the crux slopers then exit the roof instead of traversing across it, to patina edges and a jug.

481 The Lamprect Problem V11 ** Start in the same place as Pigpen, move right immediately onto sloping roof huecos. Climb straight through the roof bowls and out, traverse the sloping lip to a jug way left.

482 Struthers Problem V6 Sit start on the right side of the roof at small sloping gastons. Bust out on slopers and along the sloping lip and over.

483 Unnamed V0-

The Asteroid Belt

Little Big Horn Boulder (GPS = N34° 00.824 W116° 09.290)

Walk Southeast past Manx Boulder, following a sandy wash that leads to the small formation in the open desert (500 yds.). Map p134

484 Anaconda Wink V0 Climb over a low bulge to a slabby arete.

485 Smoke Detector V3 A lunge problem on a slab! How's that.

486 Unnamed V5 * Technical edges up to a plate on an 85° wall.

487 Little Big Horn V0- * Very steep jugz.

488 Unnamed V4 A short crimp and crank problem. Sit start under the
    roof to cracked patina.

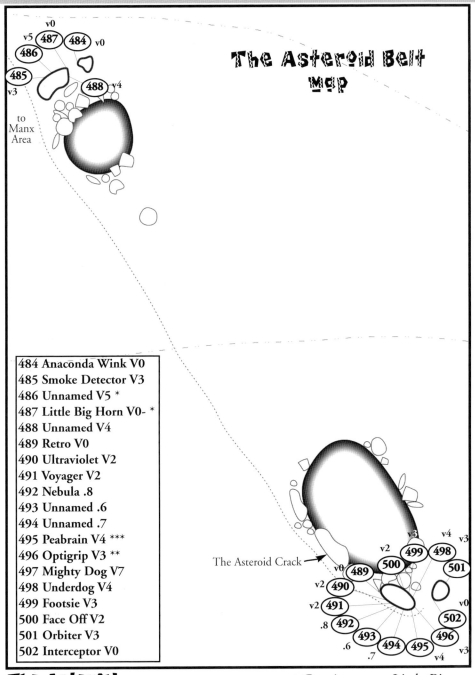

The Asteroid Belt
Map

to
Manx
Area

The Asteroid Crack

484 Anaconda Wink V0
485 Smoke Detector V3
486 Unnamed V5 *
487 Little Big Horn V0- *
488 Unnamed V4
489 Retro V0
490 Ultraviolet V2
491 Voyager V2
492 Nebula .8
493 Unnamed .6
494 Unnamed .7
495 Peabrain V4 ***
496 Optigrip V3 **
497 Mighty Dog V7
498 Underdog V4
499 Footsie V3
500 Face Off V2
501 Orbiter V3
502 Interceptor V0

The Asteroid (GPS = N34° 00.712 W116° 09.072) Continue past Little Big
Horn to the next small formation (400 yds.), the stunning Asteroid Crack is
a good landmark.
489 Retro V0 Edges and plates up a short face.

490 Ultraviolet V2 Edges and thin, black fins.

491 Voyager V2 Start at the v-slot and pull the small crimpy face.

492 Nebula .8 Plates and black knobs.

493 Unnamed .6 Crack line to a large black jug.

494 Unnamed .7 A large flake.

495 Peabrain V4 *** A vertical, thin tips crack that turn into a pumpy lieback corner.

496 Optigrip V3 ** Start at Peabrain, but move right to a slotted seam and up to thin crimps.

497 Mighty Dog V7 Start at the dish and move right into Underdog, essentially sending Underdog without a cheatstone.

498 Underdog V4 Use a cheatstone to access a high crimp, straight up to a flake.

499 Footsie V3 Start at a low foot rail to high edges.

500 Face Off V2 A steep slab with small black knobs.

Interceptor Boulder Map p134

501 Orbiter V3
Traverse all the way around the boulder on all varieties of climbing.

502 Interceptor V0
Cracks, plates and jugs on a short vertical face.

Photo: R. Miramontes

Aron Couzens on So High

Chapter

12

Real Hidden Valley 1

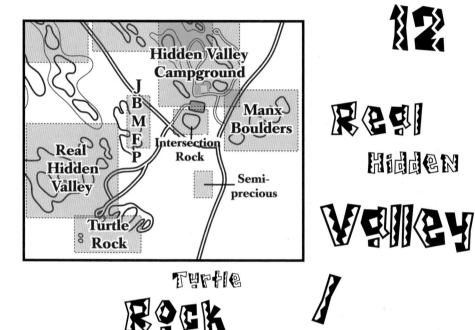

Turtle Rock

Real Hidden Valley

This area has many fine problems worth checking out. The tall and scary Betty Joe, the funky sloper traverse Kirkatron, and big dyno's on Saturday Night Live. From the West Entrance, travel 8.8 miles to the intersection and turn right, park at the bend. Restroom facilities can be found here. Map p18, 138

Turtle Rock Circuit

Another circuit masterminded by Bachar, this area has many serious highball problems, the infamous leg breaker So High, the intriguing contrasts of Shipwreck and Fistfull of Walnuts, pure fun on Block Party, and the wild scary ride on Digitalis Destructi. From the West Entrance, travel 8.8 miles an intersection, turn right and follow the road to the bend and park.Restroom facilities can be found here Map p18, 142

503 Stand Up for your Rights V0 *
504 Caesar's Palace V6
505 Sign Problem V0
506 Entrance Problem V6 *
507 West Face .7
508 Descent Route .6
509 Betty Joe Yablonski V0 R ***
510 Trailblazer V2
511 Lobster Lieback V6 *

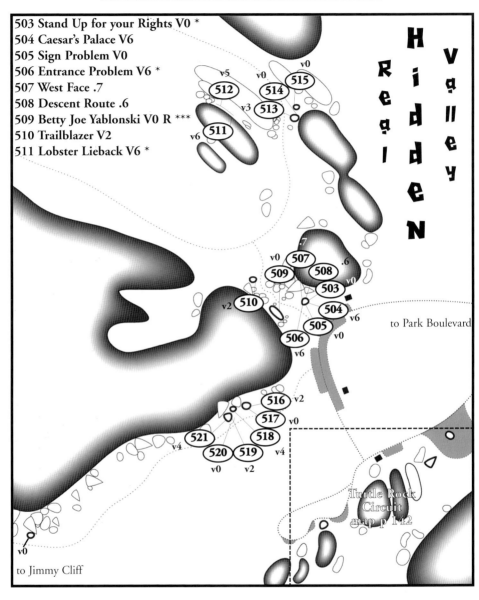

512 Kirkatron V5 ***
513 Showstopper V3 **
514 Eppie Problem V0
515 J.B. Supreme V0-
516 Soft Pretzel V2

517 Casaba V0+
518 John Glenn V4
519 Night Train V2
520 Night Crawler V0
521 Saturday Night Live V4 **

Entrance Boulder (GPS =
N34° 00.749 W116° 10.105) Map p138

**503 Stand Up for your Rights
V0 *** A short arete with a
diagonal crack.

504 Caesar's Palace V6
Run-n-jump to a long rail.

505 Sign Problem V0
Balance up dishes to edges.

506 Entrance Problem V6 *
Start at a grainy crimp and do
a huge lock off to a sidepull

flake.

507 West Face .7 Tall slab.

508 Descent Route .6 A low
angle slab, also the decent.

509

Betty Joe (GPS = N34° 00.746 W116° 10.114)
Map p138
509 Betty Joe Yablonski V0 R * A funky
move up to a small roof leads to jugs
(that are somehow not as good as you
hoped) up to a big flake.

Trailblazer Follow the entrance trail as
it winds through the boulders. Trailblazer is
on the left just before you come into the
open. Map p138
510 Trailblazer V2 Start at a high flake to a
shallow rail way over the top.

Sports Challenge Rock (GPS = N34°
00.852 W116° 10.145) Follow the entrance trail,
turn right at the sign and go 50 yds. to the
formation on th left, Kirkatron is on the
north side. Map p138
511 Lobster Lieback V6 *
Sit start on a big flake, eek out barndoor
moves up to big rails.
512 Kirkatron V5 *
A 30 ft. traverse with varied and
interesting moves. Start up a wide crack,
then traverse left either high or low, on
edges, ledges, jams, crimpers, and
slopers.
513 Showstopper V3 *
A slightly overhung arête with sidepulls
and slopers.

512

511

514 Eppie Problem V0
515 J.B. Supreme V0-
　Sit start at a big, hollow flake. Go straight up to a horizontal, slightly left, then up.
516 Soft Pretzel V2
　A long flake to a slopey mantellip.
517 Casaba V0+
　A committing mantel over a sloped landing.
518 John Glenn V4
　High underclings to a black knob, finishing with a grainy top.

Saturday Night Live Boulder (GPS = N34° 00.696 W116° 10.113)

Map p138

519 Night Train V2 A slabby face with a sidepull flake.

520 Night Crawler V0 A friction/balance traverse across a sloping shelf (which is actually a waterline from an ancient lake, that can be seen all throughout the area), with a cholla right under the crux, inspiring you to not fall!

521 Saturday Night Live V4 **
　A low horizontal on the right, a high, sloping sidepull on the left, and a wild throw for a sloping dish.

Turtle
Rock   Circuit

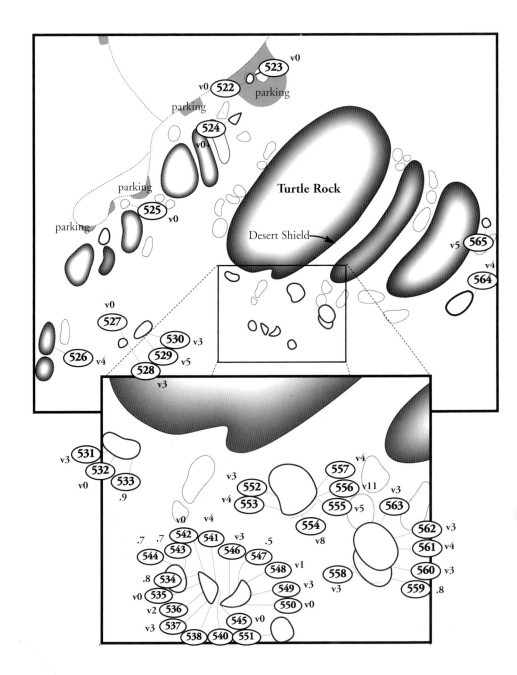

The Hat (GPS = N34° 00.669 W116° 10.039) Located in the parking lot... literally! Map p142

522 Sprinting Jew V0- Run up the slab.

523 Creeping Jew V0+ Traverse all the way around the boulder on the sloping shelf (another example of the ancient waterline) no hands at the low part by the tree.

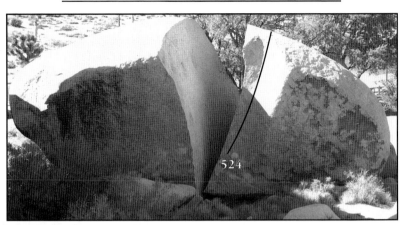

Broken Egg (GPS = N34° 00.665 W116° 10.037) Map p142
524 Act of Contrition V0+ R * A 18 ft. tall, clean arete with a big move at the end.

Discount Dyno (GPS = N34° 00.652 W116° 10.092) Map p142
525 Discount Dyno V0 A low horizontal crack with jugs to slopers.

The Cluster (GPS = N34° 00.587 W116° 10.156) Map p142
526 Digitalis Destructi V4 R * Climb a hand and finger crack out a small roof bulge, up to a right traversing thin rail.

Black Velvet Boulder (GPS = N34° 00.572 W116° 10.120) Map p142
527 Classic Curl V0+ *** A tall face/arête with tite patina rails.
528 Black Velvet V3 ** Climb a beautiful,20 ft. tall black streaked slab.

Jump Chump Map p142
529 Jump Chump V5 * Run up the face and jump to a lippy sidepull on
the left side of a giant patina plate.
530 Yawning Flare V3 Grovel a flaring crack onto a slab/ramp.

Flakey Boulder

Map p142

531 Flakey Boulder Left
V3 Thin plates and loose scabs on a steep slab.

532 Flakey Boulder Center
V0+ Edging up thin plates and loose scabs.

533 Flakey Boulder Right
.9 Plates and scabs.

Wedge Boulder (GPS = N34° 00.586 W116° 10.040) Map p142

534 N.W. Arete .8 ** Climbs a 20 ft. high, low angle arête.

535 Turtle Face Left V0 *
A 20 ft. tall slab with polished edges and glassy smears finishing just left of the point.

536 Turtle Face Center V2 *** A 20 ft tall slab with polished edges and glassy smears finishing just right of the point.

537 Turtle Knob V3 A short crimp and sloper problem.

538 Right Arete V0- A low angle lip traverse.

539 Decent Route .7 A low angle slab up to steepening plates.

540 Wedgie V3 Climb over a small bulge on edges.

541 Blood Mantel V4 Mantel over a bulge on slopers.

542 Placebo V0 Start with an awkward mantel over a low bulge up to easier climbing on the tall face.

543 Unnamed .7 A very short problem with plates.

544 Unnamed .7 A very short problem with plates.

Wave Boulder Map p142

545 West Arete V0- * Climbs a tall, clean, low angle arête.

546 March of Dimes V3 Micro edging up a tall, steep slab.

547 Decent Route .5 The ramp/arête.

548 Morning Glory V1 ***
Climb a short overhanging face/arête with nice moves.

549 Accomazzo Face V3
Pull over a low bulge and climb the 20 ft. tall face on small edges.

550 South Face V0+

Turnbuckle Map p142

551 Turnbuckle V3 * Start at a high undercling (harder if you are short), paste and lock to a sloper out left, then mantel.

So High Boulder (GPS =
N34° 00.594 W116° 10.025)
Map p142

552 Sorta High V3
Friction up into the bowl, then exit straight up the concave face. 25 ft. high friction moves.

553 Button High V4 *
An awkward mantel (of sorts) off a huge flake/chunk, traversing left to black knobs and finishing on Sorta High.

554 Powerband West V8 *
Sit start on the left side, pull sharp plates traversing right finishing just short of So High. Used to go all the way to So High but holds have broken, and has'nt been re-established.

555 So High V5 R ** A cheatstone grants you access to patina flakes at the base of a 30° overhanging crack. Thin holds and jugs up to a flaring groove/arête. Dangerous and committing moves turning onto the slab 25 ft. OTD.

556 So High (sit) V11 R * Sit start at low plates 6 ft. left of So High and power thin crimps up the 30° wall joining so high at the base of the crack. Unfortunately, holds continue to crumble.

557 Crank City V5 ** Holds may have broken on this variation start to So High.

The Shipwreck Map p142

558 Shipwreck V3 R ** Heel hook along the 60° overhanging, sloping arête. Finishes all the way around before turning over.

559 Unnamed .8 Patina cracks and plates on a short slab.

560 Fistfull of Walnuts V3 ** Stem and jam the flaring chimney/roof crack out to an edge and a sloper mantel.

561 Neoflange V4 A barndoor arête/rail, up to edges.

562 Turboflange V3 Hollow plates on a vertical wall.

563 Block Party V3 *** Jump to a blocky undercling and climb a huge, overhanging flake with jugs.

Unnamed Boulder Map p142

564 Unnamed V4 Start at low horizontal jugs, reach out the roof to flakes and slopers, to rotten jugs, jump off.

Egghead (GPS = N34° 00.608 W116° 09.911) Map p142

565 Egghead V5 Start at a sloping edge, fire up to a knob, then over on slopers.

Photo: K. Powell

Boone Speed airborn on Jump Chump

Semi-precious

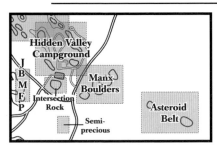

Chapter 13

Planet X

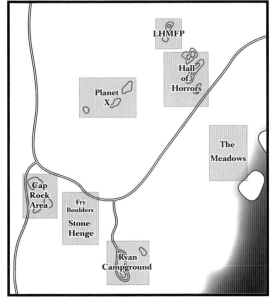

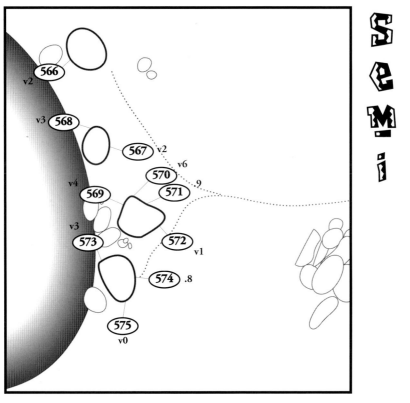

566 Zinger V2
567 Dish Mantel V2/3
568 Elagant Melon (aka; The Coke Machine) V3
569 Shite Rail V4
570 Shite Arete V6

571 Fat Flake .9
572 Belly Roll V1 *
573 El Dave V3
574 Hot and Juicy .8
575 Semi-Precious (aka; Poormans Stemgem) V0+ **

Semi-Precious

This small boulder pile has several fun easier problems, and several terrible harder ones. From Intersection Rock travel southeast .2 miles and park. The boulders are on the right. Map p18, 152

Zinger Map p152

566 Zinger V2 A shallow, diagonal thin crack to a nice pair of jugs.
567 Dish Mantel V2/3 Jump and mantel the obvious dish.

The Coke Machine (GPS = N34° 00.739 W116° 09.751) Map p152

568 Elagant Melon (aka; The Coke Machine) V3 A sloper crank on a grainy arête.

569 Shite Rail V4 Climb left along a dike/rail with poor rock.

570 Shite Arete V6 Sit start at a low dish, power over a short, grainy arête to a knobby dike.

571 Fat Flake .9 Climb a fat, slabby flake that ends with some convenient knobs.

572 Belly Roll V1 * A short, overhanging rail/crack that angles right, manteling onto the slab.

Semi-Precious (GPS = N34° 00.731 W116° 09.748) Map p152

573 El Dave V3 Start at a high, sloping, black plate. Fire up to slopes.

574 Hot and Juicy .8 A 17 ft. tall, plated out crack to a sloper top.

575 Semi-Precious (aka; Poormans Stemgem) V0+ **

A friction stemming problem up a concave face.

© G. Epperson

Evan Richards on Planet X

Planet

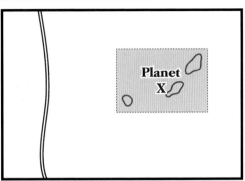

Planet X

Yet another of Bachar's visions, the Planet X circuit is full of tall scary problems including one of the all time great dyno problems, Planet X. From Intersection Rock travel southeast 1.1 miles and park. The boulders are to the east, look for the Access Fund trail. Map p18, 156

The Wood Block (GPS = N33° 59.789 W116° 09.454) Follow the Access Fund trail to the formation, go left around the formation to the boulder. Map p156

576 Mahogany V2
A painful little %@$#! barndoor arête.

577 Woody Problem V4
Delicate stemming up a near-holdless concave face.

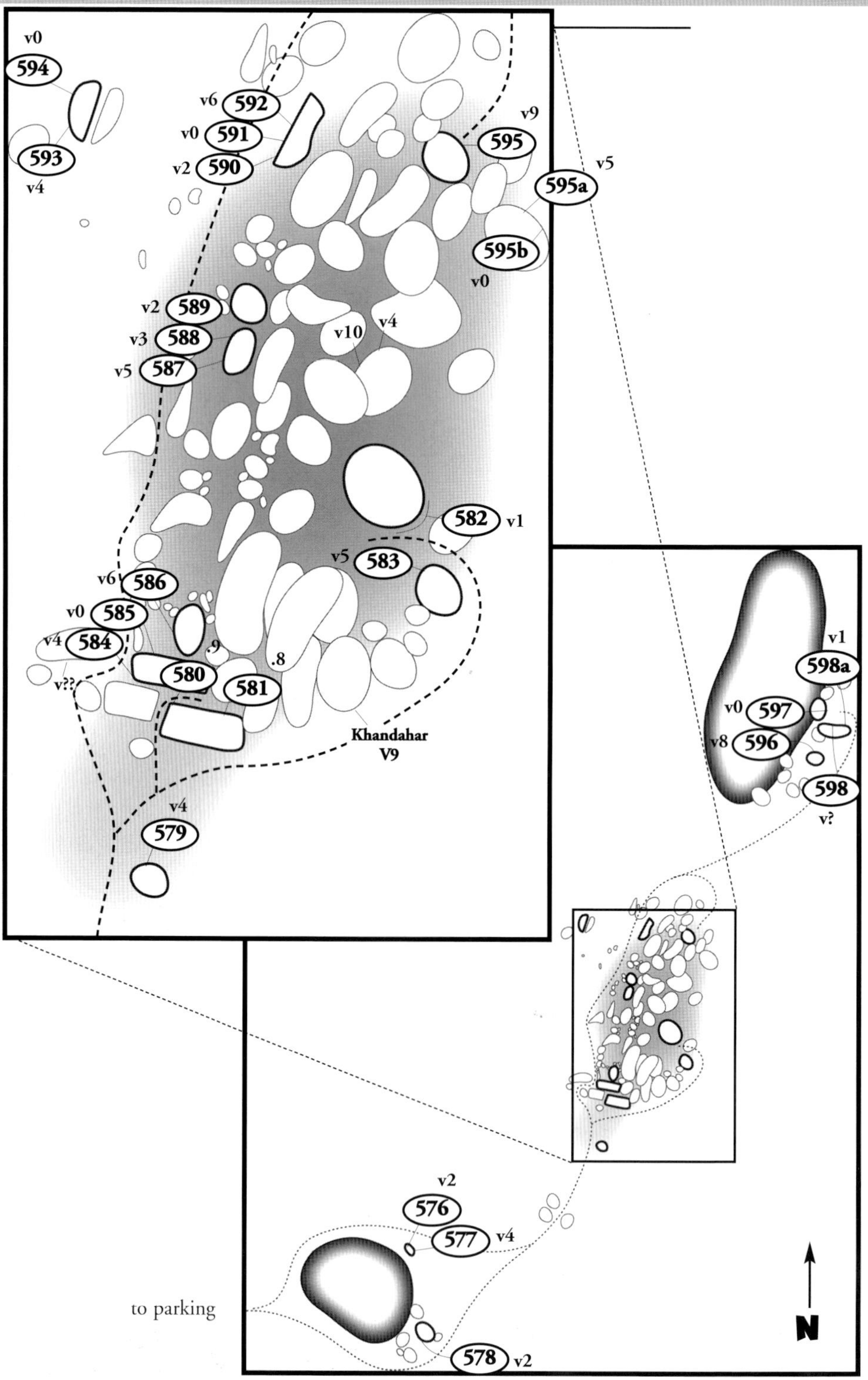

v0
594

v6 592
v0 591
v2 590
593
v4

v9
595
595a
v5

595b
v0

v2 589
v3 588
v5 587

v10 v4

582 v1
v5 583

v6 586
v0 585
v4 584
v?? 580
.9 581
.8

Khandahar
V9

v4
579

v1
598a
v0 597
v8 596
598
v?

v2
576
577 v4

to parking

578 v2

N

The Love Nest (GPS = N33°
59.751 W116° 09.483) Follow the
Access Fund trail to the
formation, go right around to the
back, Snakecharmer lies near the
base of the large spire. Map p156
578 Snakecharmer V2 A 20+ ft.
  tall slab with grainy friction
  and rotten flakes.

Newtons Law (GPS = N33°
59.752 W116° 09.372) Follow the trail
past the Love Nest as it turns to the left. Walk between boulders to a lone
boulder 100 ft. before the next small formation. Map p156
579 Newton's Law V4/5 * Start at a high jug and pound out tough sloper
moves. **Var:** start low on sloping crimps and grimp to the jug **V8**.

OK Corridor (GPS = N33° 59.791 W116° 09.372) Walk past Newtons Law and straight into the boulder pile, turn right into the Corral. Map p156

580 Alright Arete .9 R *
   A tall, slabby arête.
581 OK Face .8 Patina edges on a slab.

X Spire (GPS = N33° 59.769 W116° 09.332) From Newton's Law go around the right side of the formation until you see a large spire, this is the Planet X Spire. Map p156

582 Planet Traverse V1 15 ft. traverse with micro edging for feet.
583 Turbolator V5 * A wavy, steep slab, starting with a cheatstone at an arête and moving onto the face.

Schooly Penis (GPS = N33° 59.777 W116° 09.369) Walk past Newton's Law and to the left side of the formation, wind through boulders to this little cove. Map p156

584 Unnamed Arete V4 Climb a short, punchy arete.
585 Boulder Crack V1* A short, overhanging thin hand crack.

586 Schooly Penis V6 *Use cheatstone to start at base of a high dihedral. Toss and throw up the twin arête/dihedral, moving right to the upper arête.

The Satellite (GPS = N33° 59.800 W116° 09.337) Map p156

587 Satellite Boulder Right V5 R * Hanging jugs up and right to thin crack holds and grainy plates.

588 Satellite Boulder Left V3 R **** Hanging jugs up to a juggy vertical wall, traversing left to a balancy and tall finish. Excellent granite.

589 Traverse V2 A 12 ft. overhanging traverse on flakes and hollow plates.

PlaNet X (GPS = N33° 59.824 W116° 09.304) Map p156

590 Lucky Star V2 R ** Climbs a 20 ft., slightly overhanging face on crozzly little crimps. Sustained.

591 Wormhole V0+ R ** The obvious wide crack. Climbs more like a face with mostly positive holds.

592 Planet X V6 R ***** Start off a large cheatstone up to high gaston slopers, traverse right and up to thin crimps, then launch up the tall vertical wall to a huge bucket, finishing over on fair slopers. 22ft. tall.

Jerry's BouIder (GPS = N33° 59.830 W116° 09.353)Located 100 yds West of Planet X, on the west face. Map p156

593 Jerry's Kids V4 ** Start at the obvious thin rail, mantel onto the faint shelf and traverse right on thin holds, then up to bigger holds.

594 Telethon V0 A 16 ft. tall friction problem.

Font Problem Walk past Planet X and around the end of the formation, the problem is visible from the path. Map p156

595 Font Problem V9 A flat rail at head height to a heinous sloper topout.

595a X-Men V5 R * ** Start at a large pinch 6 ft. up, move left and up on diagonal cracks to thin edges and a grainy arete. It is also possible to go straight up at the top (V2).

595b Triple Entendre V0 R * Not one, not two, but three textbook mantels, each one slightly easier, yet slightly more comitting.

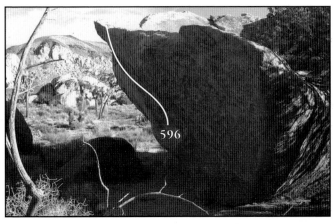

The Hang

(GPS = N33° 59.872 W116° 09.216)
Walk past planet X to the next small formation, go around the right side. Nicole Overhang is on the backside of a boulder, with the obvious Illicit Sweetie just past. Map p156

596 Nicole Overhang V8 * A thin, 25° overhanging seam to a sharp lip.

597 Illicit Sweetie V0 * ** Climb along the left edge of the 18 ft. tall face.

598 The Real Slam Dunk V?? Run and jump off a small shelf to a sharp lip. An easier variation exists 5 ft. to the right.

598a The Halfling V1 A grainy arete with slopers.

Photo: K. Powell

Kurt Smith on All Washed Up

Chapter 14

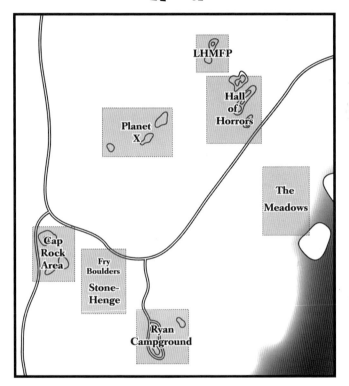

Cap Rock

Cap Rock
Highlights on this circuit include the JTree classic-Pumping Monzonite, and the Sandy Wash Corridor with many crimpfests over sand including another classic-All Washed Up. From Intersection Rock travel Southeast 1.6 miles and turn right, follow the road around the bend and park in a large parking lot on the left.
Map p 18, 164

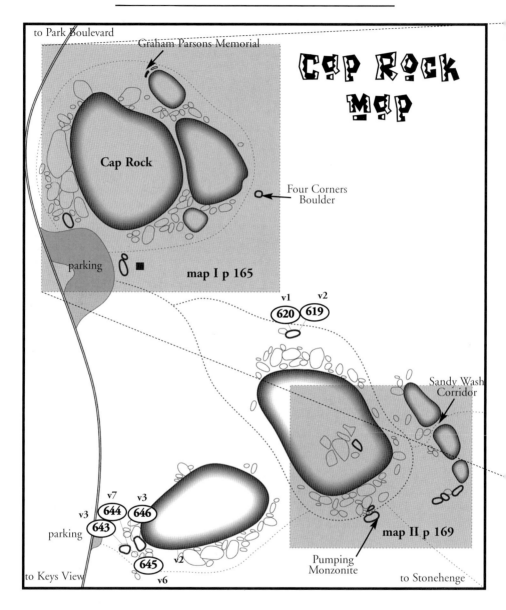

to Park Boulevard

Graham Parsons Memorial

CAP ROCK MAP

Cap Rock

Four Corners Boulder

parking

map I p 165

v1 v2
620 619

Sandy Wash Corridor

v7 v3
644 646
v3
643
parking

645
v2
v6

map II p 169

Pumping Monzonite

to Keys View

to Stonehenge

619 Herbivore V2
620 Coliherb V1 **
643 Powell Pinch V3 *

644 Powell Crank V7
645 Fitness V6
646 Up 40 V3 X **

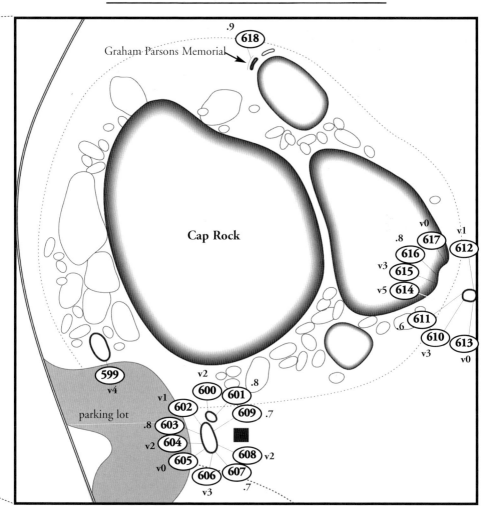

599 Parking Lot Crank V4 *
600 French Roast V2 **
601 House Brew .8
602 Sombrero V1 *
603 Fedora .8
604 Turban V2
605 Ten Gallon V0
606 Panama V3
607 Unnamed .7
608 Fez V2
609 Unnamed .7

610 West Corner V3
611 North Corner .6
612 East Corner V1
613 South Corner V0
614 High Heeled Sneakers V5
615 Love Handles V3
616 White Crack .8
617 Short Crack V0
618 Graham Parsons Memorial
Hand Traverse .9 *

Parking Lot Boulder

Map p165

599 Parking Lot Crank V4 *
A short, powerful lieback crack over a small roof.

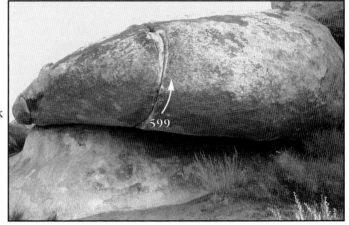

French Roast

Map p165

600 French Roast V2 ** A clean little arête problem.

601 House Brew .8 Start at the left arête and move right along the overhung lip and mantel over.

The Hatrack Map p165

602 Sombrero V1 * Climbs a slippery, cracked patina patch to a rounded summit.

603 Fedora .8 A pure friction slab. Also challenging to run up.

604 Turban V2 Friction climbing up dishes.

605 Ten Gallon V0 Friction climbing up dishes

606 Panama V3 Balance moves up a steep slab to hein slopers.

607 Unnamed .7 Traverse up the patina'ed out diagonal crack.
608 Fez V2 A curved, grainy flake up to edges and slopers.
609 Unnamed .7 Jugz and a crack.

Four Corners Boulder

This boulder is very reminiscent of the Gumdrop at Echo. Map p165
610 West Corner V3 A short technical arête with crimps and edging.
611 North Corner .6 also the decent.
612 East Corner V1 Another slabby buttress with slopes.
613 South Corner V0 Friction up the slabby buttress/arête.

Cap Rock Map p165
614 High Heeled Sneakers V5 Climbs a desperate flaring thin crack on a
  slick low angle face.

615 Love Handles V3 A high sloper/rail up to dishes.

616 White Crack .8 Climbs a clean thin crack in slick granite up a low angle face.

617 Short Crack V0 A short juggy crack, traverse off right.

Graham Parsons Memorial Located on the Northwest side of the massive Beaver Boulder. Beneath this boulder is the memorial to Graham Parsons, musician. Map p165

618 Graham Parsons Memorial Hand Traverse .9 * Traverse right, along the overhanging lip of a giant "broken off" flake for 25 ft.

Coliherb (GPS = N33° 59.324 W116° 09.749) Map p164

619 Herbivore V2 Climb the left side of a bulging, slabby arête.

620 Coliherb V1 ** Start at a bucket on the right side of the face. Climb rails angling left and up to a cruxy sloper topout.

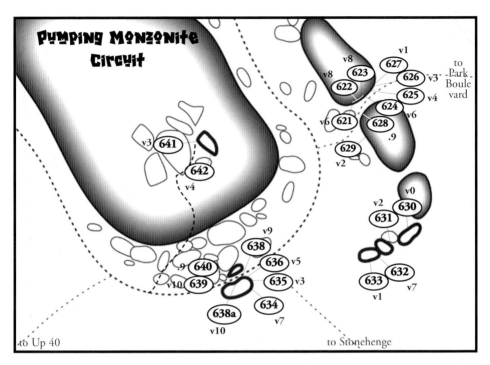

621 All Washed Up V6/7 ****
622 All Burned Out V8 **
623 Bald Eagle V8 **
624 Soar Eagle V6 **
625 Lunge Direct V4
626 Lunge for It V3 **
627 Warm Up V1
628 Slacker .9*
629 Up 20 V2 * R
630 False Ayatollah V0 **
631 Vibrator V2
632 Unnamed V7

633 Groovy V1
634 Pumping Monzonite V7 ****
635 Largo Dyno V3
636 The Hueco Patch V5 **
637 Black and White V5 *
638 Lockjaw V9/10 **
638a Through the Looking Glass V10 *
639 Talon V10 **
640 South Arete V0-
641 Unnamed V3
642 Cradle Robber V4 *

Sandy Wash Corridor (GPS = N33° 59.310 W116° 09.663) Map p169

621 All Washed Up V6/7 **** Start at a low bucket/crack and crank the gently overhung face with small edges, up to grim slopes, and finally a positive bump/sloper.

622 All Burned Out V8 ** Start at All Washed Up, moving right across the center of the face, finishing at Soar Eagle.

623 Bald Eagle V8- ** Start at Soar Eagle, move left slightly and up to the horizontal crack on steep crimps. Finish same as All Washed Up.

624 Soar Eagle V6 ** Start at the obvious crimps and move right up the overhanging face. Finish left or right.

625 Lunge Direct V4 Start on thin holds and punch up to jugs on the crack and finish with the big lunge.

626 Lunge for It V3 ** Climb up to the horizontal rail, then traverse left to sloping jugs. Fire up the concave face for the sloping top.

627 Warm Up V1 Start same as Lunge for It but climb straight up.

628 Slacker .9* A tall balance problem.

629 Up 20 V2 R * A vertical, thin crack leads to a slightly overhung, flaring (grainy) O.W.

Ayatollah Boulders Map p169

630 False Ayatollah V0 ** Balance moves into the bowl, holds getting better as you go, to jugs 18 ft. up.

631 Vibrator V2 Start at a large, pointy plate, climb improbable looking moves up and right to patina plates and slopers.

632 Unnamed V7 Sit start at jugs and bearhug the grainy, overhanging arête with slopers , to a bucket over the top.

633 Groovy V1 Jump to the big, sloping dish. Toss right to more dishes and grope over in the groove.

PUMPING MONZONITE BOULDER (GPS = N33° 59.264 W116° 09.676) Map p169

634 Pumping Monzonite V7 **** Start low at a thread/undercling hueco. Sustained moves on crimps, slopes, and slots up a slightly overhanging wall.

635 Largo Dyno V3 Jump to a dish, traverse to the right and mantel over. Weird landing.

636 The Hueco Patch V5

**** Jump and stick two shallow huecos and pump slopers to the top.

637 Black and White V5 * Lockjaw was originally sent using a flexing sidepull flake up towards the top. This flake will undoubtedly break.

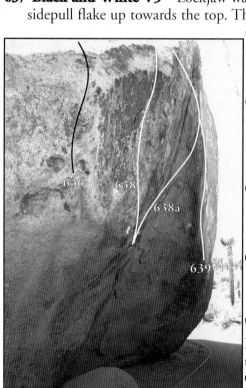

638 Lockjaw V9 ** Start leaning off of a boulder at a diagonal seam. Span the gap to the other seam and chuck for the top.

638a Through the Looking Glass V10 * Lean off the boulder to the right, stem and crank up the concave face to high jugs on the right.

639 Talon V9/10 **
Start at a sloper and climb the overhanging arête with micro edges, up to a line of buckets.

640 South Arete V0- * Climb the tall arete over the trail, roll over onto the slab higher up.

YABOLONSKI ROCK From Pumping Monzonite scramble up the formation, a little to the left. Cradle Robber can be seen from Talon. Map p169

641 Unnamed V3
Start at high sidepulls on a vertical arête, then pull on loose plates to the top.

642 Cradle Robber V4 *
A short problem up beautiful rock. Start low on small holds and climb sweet patina plates and sidepulls on a mild overhang.

Powell Boulder
Map p164

643 Powell Pinch V3 *
Traverse left on a slabby lip/arête with slopers and technical edging footwork, mantel over at the apex.

644 Powell Crank V7
You may need a cheatstone to start this one. Grim sidepull crimps and greasy

smears lead up a blunt, overhanging arête to a dish.

645 Fitness V6
Run-n-jump to a high sloper dish.

646 Up 40 V3 X **
Lean off a boulder onto the corner/shelf and crank up to a huge lieback flake. 30 ft. tall over jumbled blocks, bad from the start!

© G. Epperson

Mike Waugh on Up 40

Chapter 15

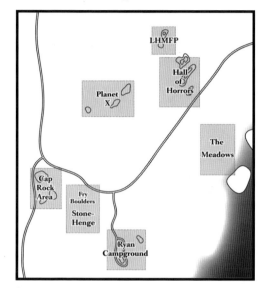

Fry Boulders

Cool orange streaked boulders right off the road, check out the sweet beta on the Fry Problem. From Intersection Rock, travel 2 miles and park in a turnout. The boulders are on the right. Map p18, 176

Stonehenge

Many interesting moderates are scattered about in this unusual rock pile, Picture Perfect being the must do. There are three possible approaches. All three are similar in distance. The first is from Cap Rock parking lot, walk the loop trail to Pumping Monzonite, then continue across the desert Eastward to a rockpile. Second is to park at Fry Boulders, walking past the Fry Boulders Southward to the rockpile. Third is to walk from Ryan Campground, past Dreaming of the Master (Westward). Map p18, 178

Fry Boulders

Stonehenge

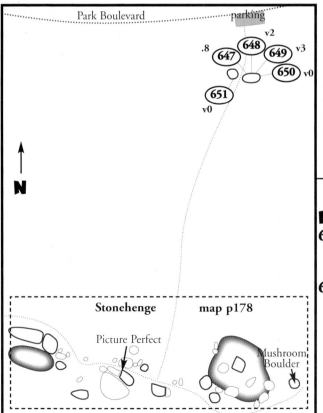

Park Boulevard · · · · · · · · · · · parking

.8
v2
647 648 649 v3
650 v0
651
v0

N

Stonehenge   map p178

Picture Perfect

Mushroom
Boulder

Fry Boulders

647 Spud Crack .8
648 Fry Problem V2 ***
649 Leap in Faith V3
650 Cornpone V0
651 Reach for a
    Peach V0 *

Fry Boulder 1
647 Spud Crack .8
Climb a juggy crack in a sculpted face.
648 Fry Problem V2 ***
Climbs a sculpted, orange vertical face. Move up and left on slopers and nice plates. Fun moves!

649 Leap in Faith V3
Run-n-jump to a very
high jug.
650 Cornpone V0
Lieback the grainy arete
651 Reach for a Peach V0 *
Friction and dishes up this
21 ft. tall boulder.
Downclimb the problem to
get off.

Stonehenge

The Rabbit Warren

(GPS = N33° 59.188 W116° 09.611)
The first boulder you encounter if you
are coming from Cap Rock.
Map p178

652 Sand Castle V3
Twin flaring cracks in a groove up to
loose jugs.

653 Leisure World V1
Start low on patina and pull funky
moves left under a small roof/
dihedral, then turn onto the slab and
jump off.

654 Fluff .8 A short, grainy, juggy arete.

655 Small World V0
Sit start this short left traversing
crack.

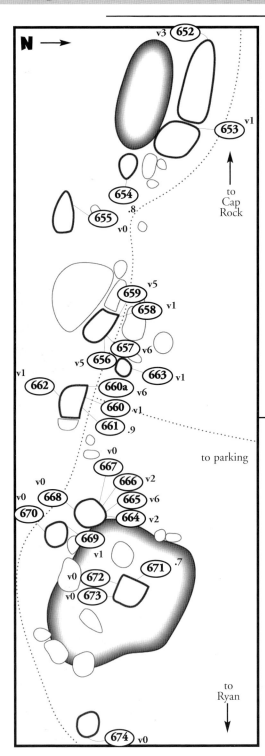

652 Sand Castle V3
653 Leisure World V1
654 Fluff .8
655 Small World V0
656 Squirm Direct V5 *
657 Squirm Right V6 *
658 Picture Perfect V1 ***
659 Picture Perfect (sit start) V5 **
660 Joker V1
660a Palm-o-Granite V6 *
661 Ace .9
662 Grainline V1
663 End of the Day V1
664 Foot Fetish V2 **
665 Prince Fari V6 *
666 Prince Hoi V2 *
667 Hoi Polloi V0
668 Multi Grain V0
669 Seven Grain Arete V1
670 Dances with Weasels V0+
671 Unnamed .7 *
672 Maverick V0
673 Renegade V0
674 Mushroom Problem V0

Picture Perfect (GPS = N33° 59.170 W116° 09.584) Map p178

656 Squirm Direct V5 * Grab a high sloper , lock that baby down, and pimp crystals straight over.

657 Squirm Right V6 * Start at the high sidepull sloper, then move right to slopers.

658 Picture Perfect V1 ** A clean little overhanging arête with thin holds.

659 Picture Perfect (sit start) V5 ** Sharp, thin crimpy.

Black Lichen Boulder

660 Joker V1 Balance moves up the tall black slab.

660a Palm-o-Granite V6 *
    Climbs a blunt arete up
    to slopers.
661 Ace .9 Easier balance
    moves up a tall black slab.
662 Grainline V1
    A nasty little grainy crack
    over a steep bulge.
663 End of the Day V1
    A very short problem, start
    at a low sidepull and a
    crimp, up to slopers.

Hoi Polloi Boulder
(GPS = N33° 59.163 W116° 09.563)
Map p178
664 Foot Fetish V2 ** Hang
    off a low jug on the lip of
    a roof and power onto the
    gorgeous patina slab. A
    little scary at the top.
665 Prince Fari V6 * Thin
    holds on glassy stone.
666 Prince Hoi V2 * Start in
    the center of the face and
    go up on patina edges.
667 Hoi Polloi V0 Climb patina jugs up and left.
668 Multi Grain V0 Grainy hollow plates and slopers.

669 Seven Grain Arete V1 Sit start to a lippy overhanging arête/lip traverse.

670 Dances with Weasels V0+ Climb the center of the slab on mostly friction with a micro flake or two.

671 Unnamed .7 * Stoney patina patches/jugs with a cool view.

672 Maverick V0 Patina flakes and jugs on a 18 ft. tall face.

673 Renegade V0 A juggy arête/face on a 20 ft. tall wall.

Mushroom Boulder

(GPS = N33° 59.160 W116° 09.527) This is the first boulder you come upon if you approach from Ryan Campground. Map p178

674 Mushroom Problem V0 A gnarly, overhanging chimney with grainy rock. Bring goggles and a bandana for this one! Downclimb chimney and jump.

Chapter 16

Ryan

Campground

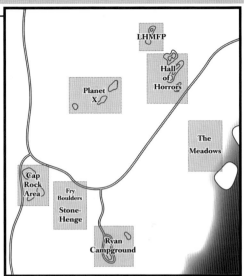

Check out
the relentless tension on Dreaming of the Master, and the
micro crimpfests on Flight Attendant and Chili Sauce. From
Intersection Rock travel Southeast for 2.2 miles and turn right onto
a dirt road. Parking in the campground loop can be scarce at times.
Map p18, 182

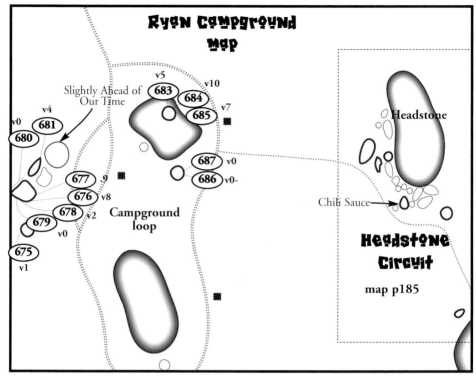

675 The Chipped Bulge V1
676 Dreaming of the Master V8 ***
677 Dreaming of the Mantel .9
678 Lip Encounter #2 V2
679 Lip Encounter #1 V0
680 Gibbs Arete V0
681 Flight Attendant V4 **

682 Flight Attendant (sit) V7 **
683 Ryan Roof Problem V5 *
684 The Love Machine V10 *
685 Gospel According to Niles V7
686 Camp Whore V0-
687 Camp Four V0

675 The Chipped Bulge V1 Start at two suspect pockets, balancy highsteps and friction. Downclimb the slab and jump.

Master Boulder (GPS = N33° 58.981 W116° 09.323) Map p182

676 Dreaming of the Master V8 *** A flaring lieback crack on a bulging face with terrible feet. A tedious sloper problem.

677 Dreaming of the Mantel .9 Jump to a knob/edge and mantel.

678 Lip Encounter #2 V2 Mantel onto a shelf and climb a tall, easy slab.

679 Lip Encounter #1 V0 Mantel onto the shelf and climb a tall, easy slab.

680 Gibbs Arete V0 A tall, clean cut lip traverse with a concrete bench nearby to add to the excitement.

Flight Attendant Rock (GPS = N33° 58.984 W116° 09.321) Map p182

681 Flight Attendant V4 ** Nasty little crimps on a sharp, overhanging arête.

682 Flight Attendant (sit) V7 ** The same as above, only more.

Roof Boulder Map p182

683 Ryan Roof Problem V5 * Climb out the small roof on a long flake.
684 The Love Machine V10 * Climb the roof flake, exiting left to slopers.
685 Gospel According to Niles V7 Traverse right along the sloping lip.

Camp Boulder Map p182

686 Camp Whore V0- Sit start on the right side of a long rail, traverse left
on buckets to an arête then topout.
687 Camp Four V0 Sit start at a bucket then climb right and up.

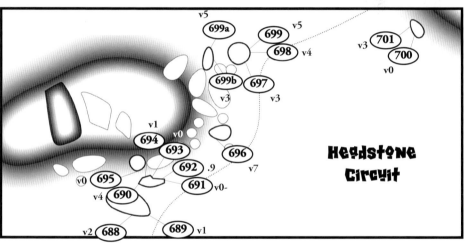

Headstone Circuit

688 Figure Five V2

689 Fidelman Arete V1 *

690 Facet Cut V4 **

691 Riffraff V0- *

692 Wannabe .9

693 Corner Problem V0 *

694 Corner Arete V1 *

695 Unknown V0

696 Chili Sauce V7 ****

697 Mattate' Face V3 *

698 Stab in the Dark V4

699 Sting in the Sun V5

699a Powers Arete V5 *

699b Powerknob V3 *

700 Stepladder Mantel V0 *

701 Arrowhead Lunge V3

FidelⱮan BoulÐer (GPS = N33° 59.042 W116° 09.150) Map p185
688 Figure Five V2 * Thin, diagonal slashes trending up and right into a bowl.

689 Fidelman Arete V1 * A juggy, overhanging buttress that is deceptively difficult.

Facet BoulÐer Map p185
690 Facet Cut V4 * ** Climbs the right side of a clean, low angle arête. Tough slopes lead to easier climbing above.
691 Riffraff V0- * Squeeze double arêtes up to a mantelshelf.
692 Wannabe .9 A balancy patina slab to a mantelshelf.
693 Corner Problem V0 * A low angle dihedral/arête up to "the mantel".
694 Corner Arete V1 Start at the corner and climb out to the right arete, reachy.

695 Unknown V0
  A short problem
  with grainy
  crimps.

Moffat Boulder
(GPS = N33° 59.037 W116°
09.141) Map p185
**696 Chili Sauce
(aka; Moffatt
Problem) V7 ****
  Climb a short
  overhanging
  dihedral to a
bulging headwall with small sloping crimps, up to slopers.

Mattate' Boulder
(GPS = N33° 59.028 W116°
09.115) Map p185
697 Mattate' Face V3 *
  Climb plates and
  slopers up a tall face.
698 Stab in the Dark V4
  Campus off slopers up
  to the sloping lip.
699 Sting in the Sun V5
  Start at a diagonal hold
  and power over on sick
  slopers.

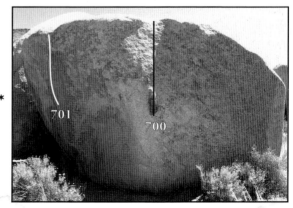

Power Boulder (GPS = N33° 59.044 W116° 09.117)
Map p185
699a Powers Arete V5 A short overhanging arete with slopers.
699b Powerknob V3 *
  Two knobs and a bulge.

The Arrowhead
(GPS = N33° 59.016 W116° 09.081)
Map p185
700 Stepladder Mantel V0 *
  A cool mantel onto a
  long, pointy black knob.
701 Arrowhead Lunge V3
  Throw off thin, grainy
  crimps.

Photo: Joe Morgan

The Author on an Underground Project

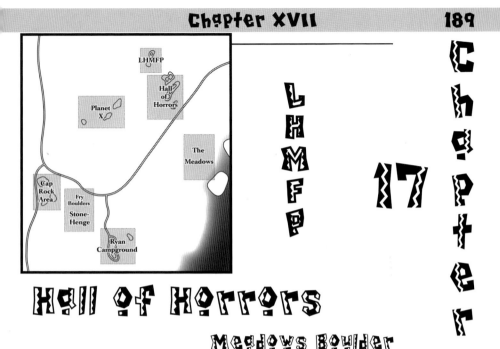

Hall of Horrors
Meadows Boulder

Meadows Boulder

This boulder has many juggy, overhanging problems. From Intersection Rock travel Southeast 3 miles (the road winds to the left and ends up going NE) and park on the right. The lone boulders are fairly obvious in the field below Saddle Rock.
Map p18, 190

Hall of Horrors

If you like 'em tall, the Cilley Cracks are for you, and the "Hall" is a stoney place to chill. From Intersection Rock travel Southeast 3 miles (the road winds to the left and ends up going NE) and park on the left, there are restroom facilities here. Access to LHMFP is from here as well.
Map p18, 192

LHMFP

Highlights in this area include the technical LHMFP, the classic Trashman Roof, and the exciting Kingpin. Park at the Hall of Horrors parking area, walk West NW past the Horrors formations, heading to the nearby Kingdome approx. .5 mile from the road.
Map p18, 196

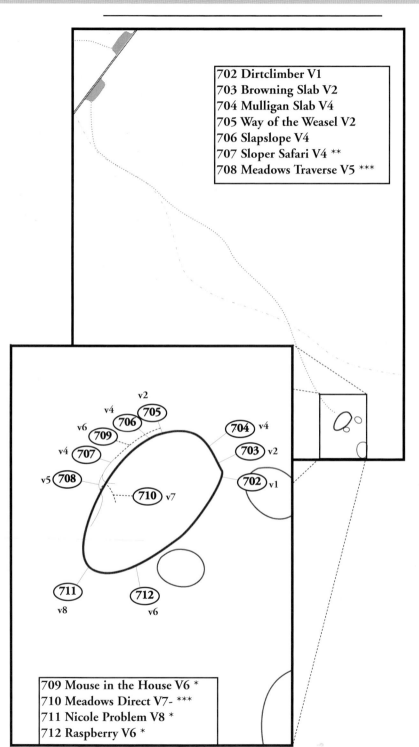

702 Dirtclimber V1
703 Browning Slab V2
704 Mulligan Slab V4
705 Way of the Weasel V2
706 Slapslope V4
707 Sloper Safari V4 **
708 Meadows Traverse V5 ***

709 Mouse in the House V6 *
710 Meadows Direct V7- ***
711 Nicole Problem V8 *
712 Raspberry V6 *

Meadows

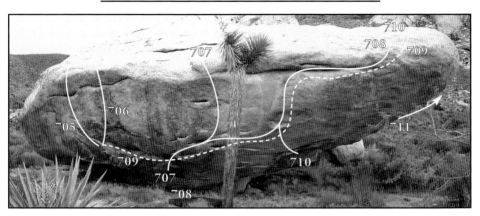

Meadows Boulder

(GPS = N33° 59.651 W116° 08.591) This rock is characterized by very steep climbing on big rounded jugs.

Map p190

702 Dirtclimber V1 Sit start at the corner and fire a move up to grainy jugs.

703 Browning Slab V2 Left side of the green slab.

704 Mulligan Slab V4 Right center of the green slab.

705 Way of the Weasel V2 Sit start on the left side of a low shelf. A big move to slot leads to a textbook mantel.

706 Slapslope V4 Sit start at the long shelf. Dyno or crimp the slot to a big slope on the right, then mantel over.

707 Sloper Safari V4 ** Sit start at low jugs and climb steep buckets up to a mailbox slot. The crux is manteling over on this one.

708 Meadows Traverse V5 *** Start the same as Sloper Safari, traverse right on steep buckets to a curved plate, fire up to the horizontal and traverse right until you come to jugs on the lip, then mantel over.

709 Mouse in the House V6 * Sit start at Way of the Weasel. Traverse right low and finish with Meadows Traverse. 30 ft. traverse.

710 Meadows Direct V7- *** Sit start at a low shelf and move left into Meadows Traverse.

711 Nicole Problem V8 * Start at two crimps about head high and crank to the diagonal crack at the lip of the overhang, traverse right and up to a jug.

712 Raspberry V6 * Sit start under the roof on underclings, slam the grainy bucket, toss out left for slopers, then onto the slab.

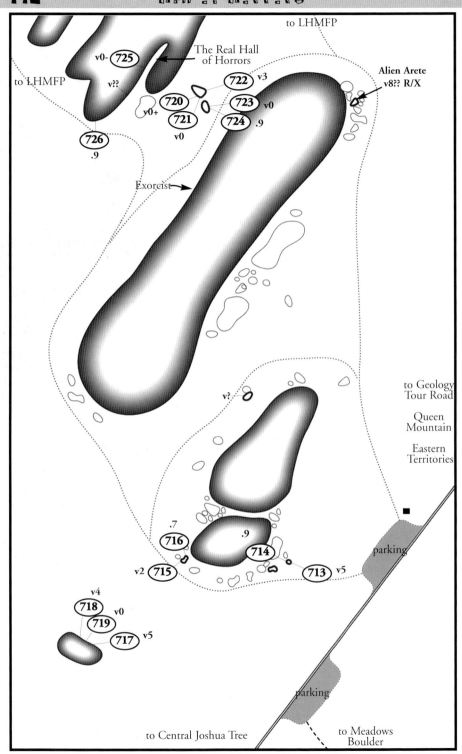

to LHMFP

v0- 725

The Real Hall
of Horrors

to LHMFP

v??

722 v3

720

723 v0

v0+

721

724 .9

v0

726

.9

Alien Arete
v8?? R/X

Exorcist

to Geology
Tour Road

Queen
Mountain

Eastern
Territories

v?

.7

716

.9

714

v2 715

713 v5

parking

v4

718

v0

719

717 v5

to Central Joshua Tree

parking

to Meadows
Boulder

713 Dwarf Toss V5
714 Lazy Day Problem .9
715 Horrors Arete V2 *
716 The Hall of Mirrors .7 *
717 Ministry of Fear V5
718 Right Cilley Crack V4 *
719 Left Cilley Crack V0 **
720 1984 is Today V0+
721 The 4th Amendment V0
722 Big Brother V3
723 Squirt V0
724 Sidekick .9
725 Walking Mexican Down
  the Hall V0-
726 Lost Lieback .9

The Dwarf
(GPS = N33° 59.849 W116° 08.786)
Map p192
713 Dwarf Toss V5 Sit start at an arete and a painful little crack hold and crank the little boulder.
714 Lazy Day Problem .9 Climbs a short lieback crack.

Horrors Boulder  Map p192
715 Horrors Arete V2 * Climb the left side of the arête, starting with a high right sidepull.
716 The Hall of Mirrors .7 * A bucketed arête on nice rock.

Cilley Rock
(GPS = N33° 59.874 W116° 08.908)
Located on a very small rockpile, 200 yds. south of the South Horrors formation. Map p192
717 Ministry of Fear V5
  A vertical wall with a high sidepull to a sick tall slab.
718 Right Cilley Crack V4 R * Climbs a thin, arching crack up a vertical to slabby 22 ft. tall face.

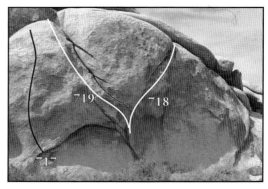

719 Left Cilley Crack V0 ** Climb a sweet curvy jam crack that goes for 23 ft..

Big Brother Boulder (GPS = N33° 00.026 W116° 08.804)

Large boulders in the middle of formations 2 and 3 . Map p192

720 1984 is Today V0+ Climbs a tall plated slab that steepens at the top.

721 The 4th Amendment V0 A tall dished out slab.

722 Big Brother V3 This problem is near the shortest corner. A vertical sloper problem.

723 Squirt V0 Start at the crack and climb right on thin patina plates.

724 Sidekick .9 Climbs a juggy crack.

The Real Hall of Horrors

A very unusual, thin corridor that goes for 100's of feet, hidden up behind the lead wall with the classic Jane's Addiction. I heard rumors of a hard traverse that goes across the base of the Jane's wall, but could not confirm it in time for print. Map p192

725 Walking Mexican Down the Hall V0- A 30 ft. traverse along a flat rail finishing at a large sidepull/corner.

Lost Lieback (GPS = N33° 00.014 W116° 08.864) Located on the Southern tip of the formation 2. Map p192

726 Lost Lieback .9 Climbs a clean splitter onto a slab.

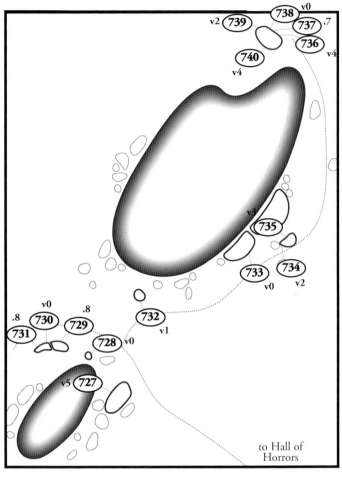

to Hall of
Horrors

727 **Kingpin V5 R** **	734 **Alfalfa V2**
728 **Pygmy V0**	735 **Buckwheat V3**
729 **Blurb .8**	736 **Death Spiral V4** **
730 **Solitaire V0** **	737 **Easy Flake .7**
731 **Fish .8**	738 **Hard Flake V0**
732 **The Simpleton V1** *	739 **Lounge Act V2**
733 **Trashman Roof V0- R** ***	740 **LHMFP V4** ***

KINGPIN

Map p196

**727 Kingpin V5 R ** A 22 ft. tall, slightly overhanging patina face up to a dish. Grainy rock.

728 Pygmy V0 A ridiculously short overhanging face with 1 crimp move to the lip.

Split Boulder

(GPS = N33° 00.156 W116° 09.002)

Map p196

729 Blurb .8 Dishes and friction on a black streaked slab.

730 Solitaire V0 ** Balance moves up sloping shelfs.

731 Fish .8 Balance up slopes to thin crack.

Simpleton Rock

Map p196

732 The Simpleton V1 * A thin crank up to a juggy, diagonal crack.

Trashman Roof

(GPS = N33° 00.189 W116° 08.954)

Map p196

733 Trashman Roof V0- R ***
A sweet hand crack starting in a small roof 10 ft. up, above a slab, and finishing OTD.

Little Rascal Rock Map p196
734 Alfalfa V2 A thin, diagonal crack in a vertical wall.
735 Buckwheat V3 Start off a low shelf and climb faint dishes and friction.

Lynn Hill Memorial Boulder
(GPS = N33° 00.223 W116° 08.961) Walk around the right side of the formation, this large boulder sits on the desert floor. Map p196
736 Death Spiral V4 ** Climb thin crimps and plates over a slab/bulge then steeper, 18 ft. or so tall.
737 Easy Flake .7 Climb a giant, slabby flake.
738 Hard Flake V0 Start on a flat rail, fire up to the shelf and mantel.
739 Lounge Act V2 A painful (and burly) thin crack in a slab over a bulge.
740 LHMFP (Lynn Hill Memorial Face Problem) V4 *** Thin edges and flakes on a vertical wall to a rounded summit 16 ft. up.

Back Country Bouldering

New frontiers

With the explosion of popularity in bouldering, many have begun to explore the vast back country areas of JTree, as a result, many new areas and problems have been opened up. This section explores several of these new areas, Geology Tour Road and its wide open desert landscape, Queen Mountain Base with its unusual and varied stone, the almost mythical Underground, and the expansive canyons of the Valley of the Kings.

With these new wonders comes new responsibility, and extra care must be taken to minimize impact. Some of these areas lie in "day use areas",which is an endangered bighorn sheep refuge.

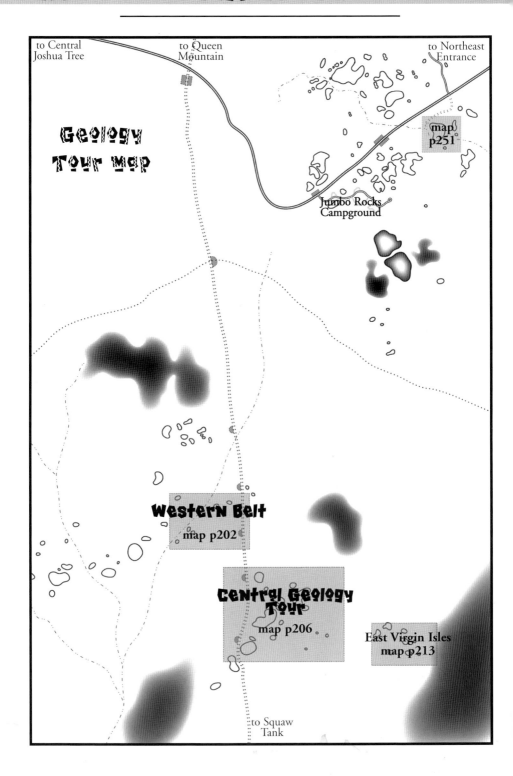

Geology Tour Map

to Central Joshua Tree

to Queen Mountain

to Northeast Entrance

map p251

Jumbo Rocks Campground

Western Belt
map p202

Central Geology Tour
map p206

East Virgin Isles
map p213

to Squaw Tank

Chapter 18

Geology Tour Road

One of the newer areas to be developed, the Geology Tour circuits are scattered across miles of open desert. The gorgeous, tall Slashface is a must do, the Tip Be Gone wall has steep jug hauling goodness, Y2k for Yosemite style granite edging, and Thin Crack for an all out battle. From Intersection Rock travel south on Park Boulevard for approx. 6.5 miles, the road will angle back North, then East through a pass between the two mountains. After several miles a dirt road will be encountered on the right. This is Geology Tour Road.

Western Belt
Travel Geology Tour Road for 3.1 miles and park in two possible turnouts on the right side of the road. Mirage is the most obvious boulder problem, facing the road. Map p200, 202

Central Geology Tour
Travel down Geology Tour Road fro 3.6 miles and park at various turnouts to access the problems scattered around near the road. Map p200, 206

East Virgin Isles
Park near the Tour Boulders approx. 4 miles down Geology Tour Road. Located approx. .75 mile East of the road. Map p200, 213

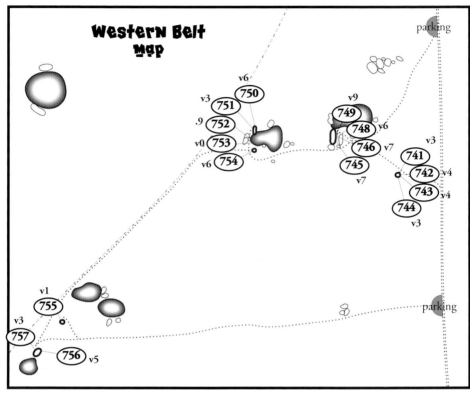

Western Belt Map

741 Rotting Crack V3/4	750 Mulligan Death Problem V6
742 Mirage V4 **	751 Mulligan Stew V3
743 Mirage Left Exit V4 *	752 Tumble Weed .9
744 Knowknob V3	753 Bruanstein Freres V0
745 Holds Be Gone V7 *	754 Pinched Loaf V6 ***
746 Tips Be Gone Traverse V7 ***	755 Purple Helmet V1
747 Hollow Flake Var. V8	756 Seam Splitter V5
748 Tips Be Gone V5/6 **	757 Slashface V3 R *****
749 Cryptic Tips V9 **	

Mirage Boulder (GPS = N33° 57.453 W116° 04.742) This boulder is clearly visible from the road. Map p202

741 Rotting Crack V3/4 A heinous grainy, overhanging, wide crack.

742 Mirage V4 ** Start on a high pinch, climb left along a horizontal crack, up to a mailslot/sloper and over.

743 Mirage Left Exit V4 * Start at the high pinch, climb left along the horizontal until the holds die out, then grope over the top.

744 Knowknob V3 Start at a flat black knob and mantel up onto the right shelf, then mantel again over the bulge.

Tips Be Gone Wall

(GPS = N33° 57.522 W116° 04.935) Located around the left side of the first rockpile, low down in a corridor. All of the problems on this wall overhang 30° with nice horizontal jugs. Map p202

745 Holds Be Gone V7 * Start at a giant flake down low and do a huge move to a seam, then fire straight up to slopers.

746 Tips Be Gone Traverse V7 **** Start Tips Be Gone, traverse left at a curved edge, then toss up to a pocketed horizontal. Finish by traversing left along the dike.

747 Hollow Flake Var. V8 Direct the finish of the long traverse by going straight up on the hollow flake.

748 Tips Be Gone V5/6 ** A low stand up start on a dike with small incuts straight up on big holds to a crimpy pull over the top.

749 Cryptic Tips V9 ** Start at the large jug on the far right side of the wall, traverse left and slightly down along crimpy seams, finishing with the long Tips Traverse.

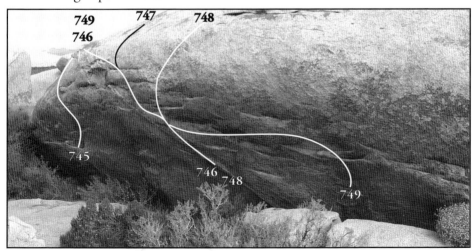

Floodzone
Located on the backside of a rockpile 500 yds. west and slightly left of tips be gone, Just before the huge wash. Map p202

750 Mulligan Death Problem V6 Sit start and send gastons and slopers up a short face with a bad landing.

751 Mulligan Stew V3 Start at a jug and climb right and up to a committing mantel over a bad landing.

752 Tumble Weed .9 Tiptoe up a faint green rail.

753 Bruanstein Freres V0 Climb grainy cracks and buckets angling left to bigger buckets. Poor rock.

Pinched Loaf
(GPS = N33° 57.368 W116° 05.143)
Located on the southside of a rockpile 500 yds. West and slightly left of Tips Be Gone, Just before the huge wash. Map p202

754 Pinched Loaf V6 *** Slopers up to a black oval knob in a small dihedral, then go big for the lip.

755 Purple Helmet V1 Climb the 20 ft. tall spire, starting on an arête and moving left onto the face.

Slash Boulder

(GPS = N33° 57.210 W116° 05.226) Best found by walking 400 yds. South down the huge sandy wash from Pinched Loaf. From the parking walk West and slightly left for approx. .4 mile, Slash Boulder sits near a small rockpile just before the huge wash.

Map p202

756 Seam Splitter V5 I have never been able to build a cheatstone high enough to get to the horizontal. Traverse the seam on the high slab.

757 Slashface V3 R ***** A gorgeous vertical face with horizontal slashes. Thin seams lead to good slots, then juggy mailslots high off the deck.

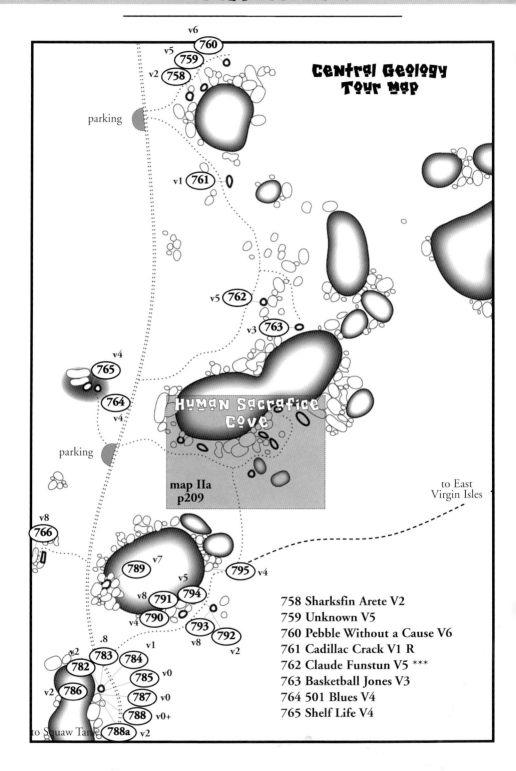

Central Geology
Tour Map

v6
760
v5
759
v2
758

parking

v1 761

v5 762

v3 763

v4
765

764
v4

Human Sacrafice
Cove

parking

map IIa
p209

to East
Virgin Isles

v8
766

789 v7

v5

795 v4

v8 791 794
790
v4
793 792
v8 v2
.8 v1
783 784
782
785 v0
v2 786
787 v0
788 v0+
to Squaw Tank 788a v2

758 Sharksfin Arete V2
759 Unknown V5
760 Pebble Without a Cause V6
761 Cadillac Crack V1 R
762 Claude Funstun V5 ***
763 Basketball Jones V3
764 501 Blues V4
765 Shelf Life V4

Sharks Fin (GPS = N33° 57.086 W116° 04.612) Map p206

758 Sharksfin Arete V2 Sit start at a fin to a grainy, overhanging arete.

759 Unknown V5 Start at thin crimps and crank the overhang.

Pebble (GPS = N33° 57.109 W116° 04.536) Map p206

760 Pebble Without a Cause V6 Campus the large black knob/pinch out left to a seam, then power over.

761 Cadillac Crack V1 R A 20 ft. tall shallow tips crack on a slab.

Funstun Boulder (GPS = N33° 56.881 W116° 04.553) Map p206

762 Claude Funstun V5 * Start at the base of a juggy flake on a steep bulge. Climb along the flake until it ends, then punch out left to a flat black knob. Balance over on black knobs.

763 Basketball Jones V3 Start at a low horizontal crack, over a bulge to a sloping shelf.

Blues Rock (GPS = N33° 56.859 W116° 04.714) Map p206
764 501 Blues V4 A low angle lieback seam with balancy moves.
765 Shelf Life V4 Start on a low jug and climb the blank, vertical face.

Y2K Boulder (GPS = N33° 56.691 W116° 04.750) Map p206
766 Y2K V8 ***

Climbs a slightly overhanging arête formed by a thick, broken flake. Thin holds along the shin bashing arête with a big move over the top to a hidden jug.

767 Ladies Helper V1
A 15 ft. tall slab with a large plate midway.

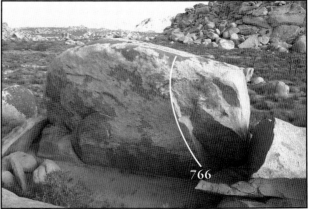

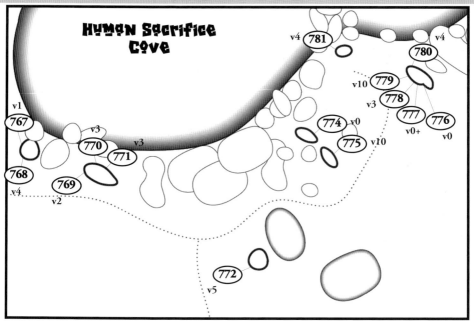

Human Sacrifice Cove

767 Ladies Helper V1
768 Melon Arete V4
769 Knuckleball V2
770 Curveball V3
771 Gutterball V3
772 Special K Crack V5
773 Special K (sit) V7
774 The Wanderer V0

775 Thin Crack V10 ***
776 Leftward Ho V0-
777 Dripper Right V0+ **
778 Dripper Left V3 ***
779 Pignose V10 **
780 Driblet V4 *
781 Puttyface V4 **

---

768 Melon Arete V4 A blunt arete.

Knuckleball Boulder
Map p209

769 Knuckleball V2 Start at a hand sized, black knob 4.5 ft. up and move onto the blunt arête and over.

770 Curveball V4 *Stem up the concave face with small knobs and faint dishes.

771 Gutterball V3 A mantel problem left of the black knobs.

772 Special K Crack V5 Climb off a boulder and out an overhang on a diagonal thin crack.

773 Special K (sit) V7 Sit start on the boulder and climb the overhanging crack.

Human Sacrifice Cove

Map p209

774 The Wanderer V0

A low flake system leads up a steepening slab to high flakes.

775 Thin Crack V10 ***

A relentless tips lieback crack on a vertical, blank face.

Dripper Boulder (GPS = N33° 56.806 W116° 04.356) Map p209

776 Leftward Ho V0-

A flaring crack up a corner/ramp finishing 20 ft. up.

777 Dripper Right V0+ **

Traverse right along a 6 ft flake under a steep wall, reach long to an upper crack angling back left above the steep wall. 16 ft. tall.

778 Dripper Left V3 ***

Start at the long flake, move left to a high lieback flake.

779 Pignose V10 ** Start at a high, perfect one hand knob on an otherwise featureless bulge to a big, black pinch high on the slab.

780 Driblet V4 * This tough little problem climbs a blunt corner 1 ft. from an arête. Balancy.

781 Puttyface V4 ** A vertical face with micro's to slopers.

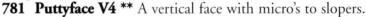

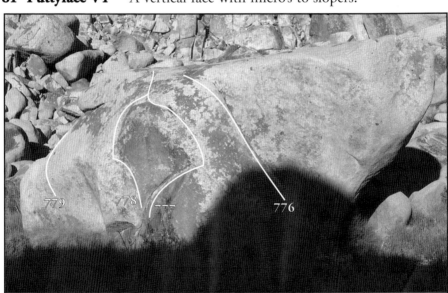

Tour Boulders

(GPS = N33° 57.098 W116° 04.715) Map p206

782 Blackdot V2 Climbs a tall slab with scabby edges to a big black patch.

783 Commando .8 The lieback crack.

784 Braided Lines V1 Climb the middle of the slab on scabby edges.

785 Bluecut V0 * Crack

786 Zot V2 Start low on a horizontal and a sidepull up to a corner.
  Bad landing.

787 Purple Microdot V0 * Climb a knobby slab.

788 Cinders V0+ * Cool knobs.

788a Rob's Prob. V2 * Step off a boulder and move up to a black sidepull.

Dark Amber

 This hard to find problem is approached by scrambling up the frontside of
the formation, and is hidden in a notch in the boulders. Map p206

789 Dark Amber V7 ** Sit start at obvious holds on the arête, move right
 and up on a gently overhanging face with thin plates. Finishes with a
sloping black knob and a jug over the top.

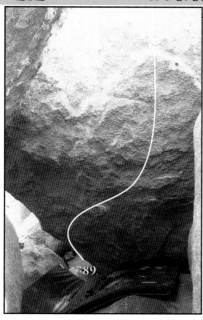

Velvet Elvis Rock

(GPS = N33° 56.564 W116° 04.647) Map p206

790 Wild Turkey V4 *

Start at a jug on the left, then throw right to a sidepull. Move into a shallow thin crack on a vertical face. Sketchy top.

791 Velvet Elvis V8 **

Start off the ground on a diagonal thin crack in a smooth vertical face leading into a dihedral. Harder to start if you are short. V4 if you lean off left boulder to start.

Dike Boulder

(GPS = N33° 56.559 W116° 04.618) Map p206

792 Cleavage V2 *

A large, thin flake going over a slight bulge.

793 Dikes with Acne V8/9 ***

Sit start at jugs on the large dike, traverse right on shallow pockets to the crack (Cleavage).

794 Dike Face V5 **

A fat dike on a slight overhang with

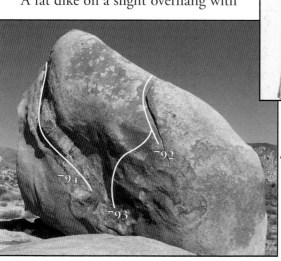

sidepull jugs and slopers up to nice crimps and knobs. Unusual stone.

795 Once Upon a Dime V4

Thin edges and friction up a steep slab to a thin crack.

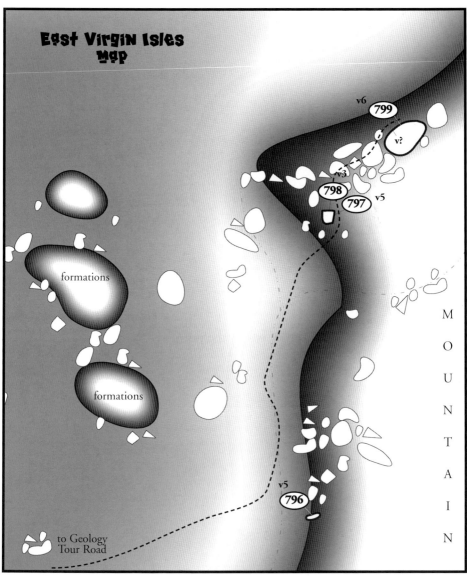

East Virgin Isles Map

796 The Jumping Bean V5
797 Can of Whoopass V5

798 Hondo Roof V3 **
799 Shipwrecked V6 **

East Virgin Isles

Walk east past Dike Wall towards the mountain for approx. .75 mile, stay to the right of any rock formations, drop down into a wash just before the mountain. Map p200

796 The Jumping Bean V5 A vertical face with a lone plate midway.

Hondo Roof

Map p213

797 Can of Whoopass V5 Sit start at the rail, climb through the center of the overhang to a jug on the left of the point.

798 Hondo Roof V3 ** Traverse a juggy rail for 5 feet under the roof then turn onto a clean, dark slab with diagonal slashes.

799 Shipwrecked V6 **

Chapter
19

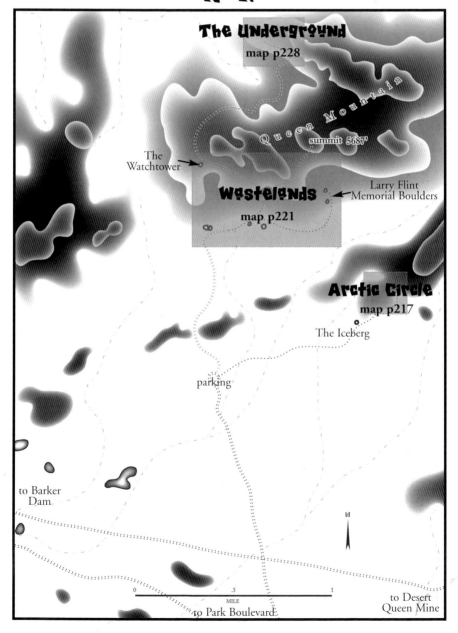

The Underground
map p228

Queen Mountain

summit 5687'

The
Watchtower

Larry Flint
Memorial Boulders

Wastelands
map p221

Arctic Circle
map p217

The Iceberg

parking

to Barker
Dam

to Desert
Queen Mine

0   .5   1
MILE

to Park Boulevard

QUEEN MOUNTAIN BASE

This area is characterized by unique and varied stone, from dark brown, glassy smooth desert varnish rock along the base of the mountain to classic josh granite peppered with black diorite knobs at the Arctic Circle. Approaches are generally long walks across flat desert. Remnants from mining and Indian pictographs can be found all throughout the valley.

Arctic Circle Cove
From the parking lot walk East along the band of small hills for approx. 1 mile, passing the obvious Iceberg, continue right along the base of the hills (passing many knobby boulders with much potential) to a canyon that leads to a small cove.
Map p215, 217

The Wastelands
From the parking lot go North, following a well travelled wash that turns into a road for approx. 1 mile, cutting through a notch in the hill, then into a valley and ending along the mountainside.
Map p215, 217

Larry Flint Memorial Boulder
These boulder are located approx. 1.5 miles from the parking, right of the summit along the base of the mountain,in the right side of two bizarre troughs etched in the mountain that run down from the top. Best reached from the Arctic Circle, go North for approx. .5 mile, the boulder and streakes in the mountain should be visible.From the end of the miner's road, pass the Habanero and drop down to flat ground, follow a large sandy wash that goes east for approx. .5 mile, and follow the right trough to the boulders.
Map p215, 217

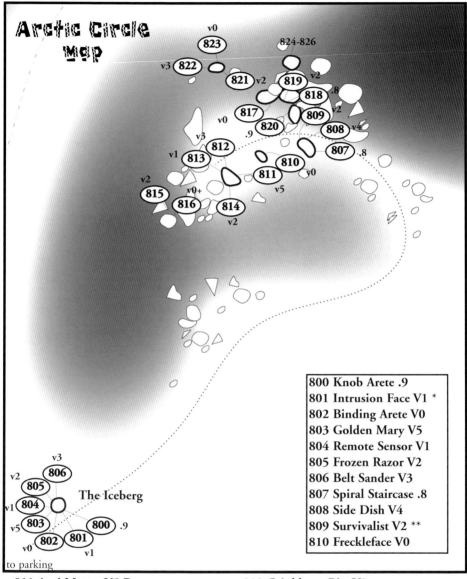

Arctic Circle Map

v0
823

824-826

v3 822

821 v2 819 v2

818 .8

817 v0 809 v2

820 808 v4

.9

v3 807 .8

v1 813 812

810

v2 811 v0

815 v0+ v5

816 814

v2

800 Knob Arete .9
801 Intrusion Face V1 *
802 Binding Arete V0
803 Golden Mary V5
804 Remote Sensor V1
805 Frozen Razor V2
806 Belt Sander V3
807 Spiral Staircase .8
808 Side Dish V4
809 Survivalist V2 **
810 Freckleface V0

v3
806
v2
805
806
v1 804
The Iceberg
v5 803
v0 802 801 800 .9
v1

to parking

811 Anti Matter V5 R	819 Crinkles-n-Bits V2
812 Particle Accelerator V3 **	820 Deuceface .9
813 The Bullhorn V1	821 Waves of Grain V2
814 Snake Eyes V2	822 Pavement V3
815 Undertaker V2	823 Roadstop V0
816 Bounty Hunter Arete V0+ *	824 Local Color
817 Stepping Stone V0 R	825 Brownian Motion
818 Black Knob .8	826 Shades of Grey

The Iceberg

(GPS = N34° 02.334 W116° 05.760) This lone square boulder is characterized by huge crystal'ed granite. Map p217

800 Knob Arete .9 Big black knobs up a slabby face.

801 Intrusion Face V1 * Small, incut black knobs up a slabby face.

802 Binding Arete V0 A 16 ft. tall, low angle arete with black knobs and plates.

803 Golden Mary V5 Grainy, thin crimps on a vertical face, out right to a thin crack and jugs.

804 Remote Sensor V1 Grainy crimps on a vertical face, out left to plates and knobs.

805 Frozen Razor V2 Gritty ass crimps over a small bulge to an 18 ft. tall slab.

806 Belt Sander V3 Gritty edges over a small bulge to an 18 ft. tall slab.

The Arctic Circle Known for the very unusual black, extrusion knobs that are spattered all over the boulders. Map p215, 217

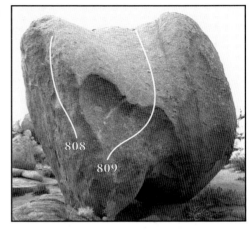

Servivalist Boulder

(GPS = N34° 02.483 W116° 05.503)
Map p217

807 Spiral Staircase .8
    Huge knobs and jugs.
808 Side Dish V4 *
    A 95° wall, starting off sidepull slopers to a juggy dish.
**809 Survivalist V2 ** ** Lean off a boulder and move right into a concave face with dope little black knobs to a high balancy finish.
810 Freckleface V0 Climb knobs up a short face.

Big Tree Boulder (GPS = N34° 02.479 W116° 05.521) Map p217

**811 Anti Matter V5 R ** ** Gaston the overhung pod up to jugs and slopers.
**812 Particle Accelerator V3 ** ** Fire up the overhanging face to a plated out crack.
813 The Bull Horn V1
814 Snake Eyes V2 A blunt, vertical arete with black slopers to a horn.
815 Undertaker V2 Pull a short overhang to a flaring crack.
816 Bounty Hunter Arete V0+ *

The Stepping Stones Map p217

817 Stepping Stone V0 R Step off a boulder and climb grainy edges up a buttress.

818 Black Knob .8 Start at a large black knob and climb a grainy slab.

819 Crinkles-n-Bits V2 Crimp up small black knobs on a short vertical wall.

820 Deuceface .9 edges over a bulge.

Asphalt Boulder

(GPS = N34° 02.520 W116° 05.553) Aptly named boulder on the ridgeline 100 ft. North of the cove. Map p217

821 Waves of Grain V2 A grainy scoop to grainy edges.

822 Pavement V3 Tiny black knobs over a bulge.

823 Roadstop V0 Black knobs up a slab.

no climbing

Pictograph Boulder (GPS = N34° 02.527 W116° 05.506) This boulder has native rock art under the roof, these three problems are off limits to climbing, please do not climb here.

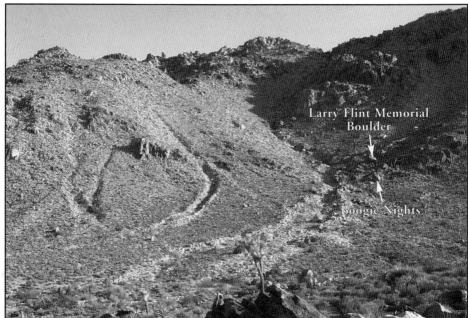

Larry Flint Memorial Boulder

Boogie Nights

824 **Local Color**
825 **Brownian Motion**
826 **Shades of Grey**

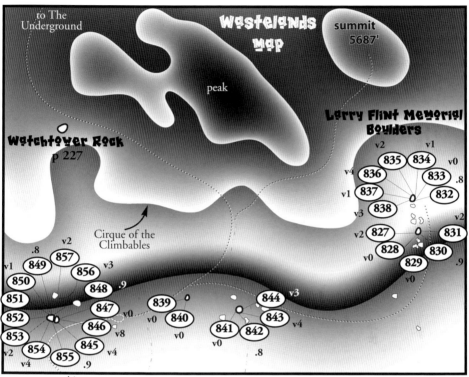

Boogie Nights (GPS = N34° 02.880 W116° 05.820) Map p221
827 Dirk Diggler V2 Thin plates over a bulge.
828 Flesh V0 Flakes up a vert. to slab face.
829 G-Spot V0 A thin, arching crack with loose plates.
830 Pornogaphy .9 Big holds up a slab.
831 The Labia V2 Pull onto the plated lip of a low overhang, to a slab.

Larry Flint Memorial Boulder Map p221
832 Unnamed .8 R * Climb gorgeous faceted blocks on low angle glassy smooth rock. Bad landing.
833 Fake Plastic Love V0 * Glassy smooth slab with unusual geometric knobs low down.
834 Swank V1 R * A vertical face right to an arete, with smooth crimps.
835 Punk V2 R * Fire the small overhang, starting at a jug, and finishing up a slab. Bad landing.
836 Hustler V4 R * Climb a short bulge to a blunt upper arete. Bad landing.
837 The Reacharound V1 R ** * Climb over a short overhang to giant plates on an upper slab.
838 Triple X V3 Thin plates up a smooth, vertical face/arete. Bad landing.

Last Call Boulder (GPS = N34° 02.758 W116° 06.262) Map p221

839 Pavlovs Dog V0 Start low and climb a thin seam to knobs and jugs on the left.

840 Positron V0 Left arching thin cracks and plates.

The Habanero (GPS = N34° 02.770 W116° 06.196) Map p221

841 Brownout V0 A vertical face with diagonal cracks and blocks.

842 Downtime .8 A short vertical face with plates.

843 Habanero V4 * Thin crimps up to a horizontal seam, traversing right to slopers and jugs.

844 Finger Food V3 A short finger crack with nice slots.

Mullet Bloc (GPS = N34° 02.707 W116° 06.522) Map p221

**845 Poker in the Front V4 ** ** Sit start at thin slots on a blunt arete, power up on glassy slopers to jugs.

846 Liquer in the Rear V8 * Sit start at a low jug and crimps, crank the bulge to pockets, joining The Three Mulleteers.

847 The Three Mulleteers V0 * Cool pockets on a short face.

848 Midnite Luvr of TriplXTC .9 * Klimes a glasee, skulptid slab with kool edjizZ.

849 Nizzle .8 * Climbs a smooth, sculpted slab.

850 Doosh V1 * Start at a low undercling, traverse the lip and pull over onto the smooth slab.

851 Its Da Oooze V2 ** Start at a low jug, climb a small bulge to crazy egdes and plates on sculpted stone.

852 The Mullet V0 ** Climbs a high lieback crack with knobs and a sweet pocket.

853 Tinkerbell's Anus V2 ** Sit start at low crimps and climb a short overhang to a sculpted slab with sweet huecos.

854 Moral Wasteland V4 ** Start at a low jug and climb the glassy smooth bulge on incut edges.

855 A Mullet, a 12 in. Cord, and a V13 Ability .9 High jugs and plates (some loose).

856 Whips, Chains, and Lox V3** Sit start at small jugs, traverse right along the overhanging lip on crimps, slopes, and jugs.

857 Tosspint V2 * Sit start at a jug, chuck out the lip to sharp crimps and sculpted jugs.

Chapter 20
The Underground

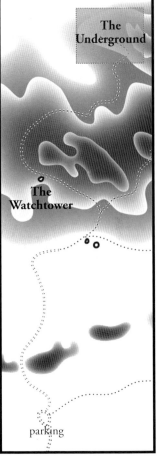

S hrouded in mystery and protected by a labrynthian approach, this area became known as a sort of local "myth". Well, myth no more, as this chapter unlocks the secret of the approach, and opens up a whole new world of stone and bouldering potential.

The Underground

Lose your perception of JTree being coarse grained, low angle climbing. Picture a world of black and orange, caramel and creme, with glassy varnish and smooth holds. Most everything is overhanging, with actual holds! This is also the largest circuit in Josh, around 100 problems in a condensed area with potential for much more. Highlights in this area: the sweeping red wall on Oldskool, the dramatic overhang on Blue, crazy OTD jugs on Altered States, the ultra smooth roof crack Presence, bizarre beta on Zen Rock Garden, sweet line of 4:20, everything on the Porcelean Wall, insane flakes on Divine Intervention, feature boulder, EVERYTHING on Eclipse Boulder, OdidImention Dark Matter, everything on 40° Wall, the sensational Have a Cigar, and the exquisite crimps of Hot Rats.

Approach

Now for the bad news, this approach can be done in 1 hour if you have it dialed and you're moving, but typically it takes most 1.5 hrs. Distance is about 2.5 miles, with an elevation gain of about 1000 ft, and involves several class 3 scrambles. From the parking lot go North, following a well travelled sandy wash that turns into an old dirt road. Follow the road

for approx. 1 mile, it will wind towards the mountain, bend to the right and then end. A large cairn marks the trail, follow the trail as it angles up the ramp/gully. Just before the top of the gully, branch left to an upper plateau, follow the plateau for 300 yds. as it angles upward, until you reach The Watchtower. Form The Watchtower, follow a faint trail that leads to the right (N), up over the summit. Walk down the backside towards the canyon, cross the canyon high up by the cliffs, then walk down an open area on dirt, when you start going downwards, turn sharp right and follow a fairly obvious trail. Continue diagonally and sideways across the mountain until you reach a steep rocky gully, drop down the gully for 200 ft. exit the gully and continue sideways, you should come out above a small cliff band, follow the trail sideways and down, passing large boulderable boulders. When you get to the base, cross the large wash and head up a smaller wash to the left. When you reach the first large boulder in the wash, head right to the base of the cliff. Climb the steep gully up to the upper tier. Walk left along the upper level for approx. 200 yds. staying out along the rocky edge. The Underground will become visible on the ridge crest.

Map p225, 228

858 Voodoo Chile V5 **
859 Left V Nothing V0+ **
860 Right V Nothing V0+ **

861 Kentucky Fried Christ V2 R ***
862 Unnamed Traverse V1
863 Electric Church V3 R **

The Watchtower

(GPS = N34° 02.996 W116° 06.185) Nearing the summit of the approach to The Underground lies this beautiful boulder, a preview of what is to come. Sitting atop this boulder is one of the finest views in all of Josh.
Map p215

858 Voodoo Chile V5 ** Start on the left side of a long rail (by a yucca), traverse right under the bulge, then surmount the bulge.

859 Left V Nothing V0+ ** Start at a low sidepull and climb the shiney brown face up and left on bomber jugs.

860 Right V Nothing V0+ ** Start at a low sidepull and climb jugs and moving into a huge flake on the right.

861 Kentucky Fried Christ V2 R *** Climb the obvious crack line going out the roof, traversing right along the roof on killer jugs, and finishing up a vertical crack. Climbs over an old nolina.

862 Unnamed Traverse V1 Start at the V Nothings and traverse right along a horizontal crack for 15 ft.

863 Electric Church V3 R ** Start at a low jug and move up left through the bulge on slopers, linking into the juggy crack over the roof.

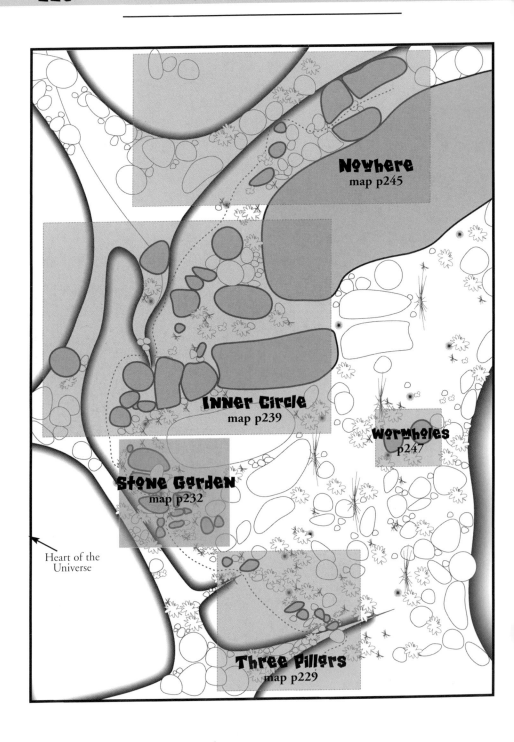

Nowhere
map p245

Inner Circle
map p239

Wormholes
p247

Stone Garden
map p232

Heart of the
Universe

Three Pillars
map p229

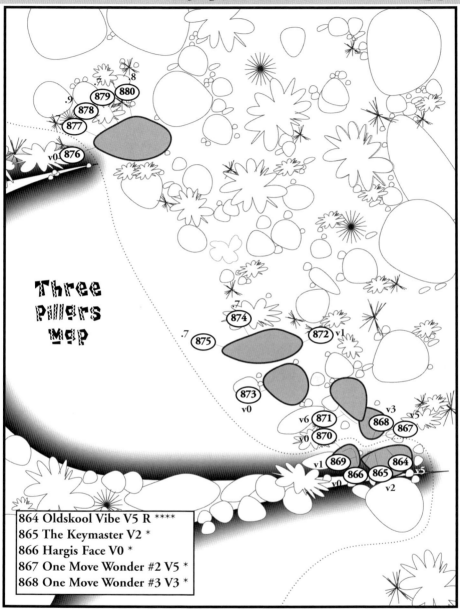

Three Pillars Map

864 Oldskool Vibe V5 R ****
865 The Keymaster V2 *
866 Hargis Face V0 *
867 One Move Wonder #2 V5 *
868 One Move Wonder #3 V3 *

869 Lochness Traverse V0+
870 Clusterfuck V0-
871 Blue V6 ***
872 Shardz V1
873 Boot Problem V0
874 Flake Route .7

875 Juggz .7
876 Rotten Apple V0
877 Descent .7
878 Dooby .9 *
879 Unnamed .7
880 Unnamed .8

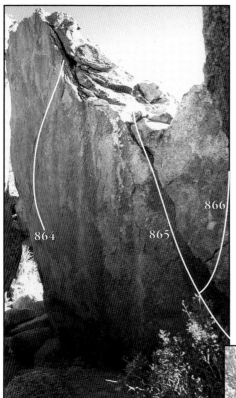

Pillar of Nobility Map p229

864 Oldskool Vibe V5 R **
Climbs a gorgeous red, gently overhanging face. Start at a thin plate/sidepull, move into a right leaning seam line.

865 The Keymaster V2 * Sit start at buckets, climb the crack only.

866 Hargis Face V0 *
Sit start at the buckets and climb straight up.

867 One Move Wonder #2 V5 *
Sit start at small incut flakes and bust a big move to the lip of the overhang.

868 One Move Wonder #3 V3 *
Sit start on small incut flakes and climb left out the short overhang.

869 Lochness Traverse V0+
Sit start and traverse the lip of the boulder right, finishing around the corner.

870 Clusterfuck V0-
A clean stemming dihedral up to a crack.

Pillar of Truth
(GPS = N34° 03.563 W116° 06.111)
Map p229

871 Blue V6 **
Jump (if your short like me) to opposing slopers on a radically steep face/arête, fire out the beautiful caramel, cream, and black streaked prow to jugs.

Pillar of Hope Map p229
872 Shardz V1
> Climbs an overhanging arête with small incut flakes.

873 Boot Problem V0
> Climb a high crack/jug/patina thing.

874 Flake Route .7
> Undercling a giant flake.

875 Juggz .7
> Climbs a jugged out arête.
> Bad landing.

Golden Nugget
(GPS = N34° 03.566 W116° 06.134)
Map p229

876 Rotten Apple V0 Climb the flakey buttress.

877 Descent .7 The ramp.

878 Dooby .9 * Clean brown patina plates on a 15 ft. low angle face.

879 Unnamed .7 A juggy 15 ft. tall crack

880 Unnamed .8 A grainy buttress/arête.

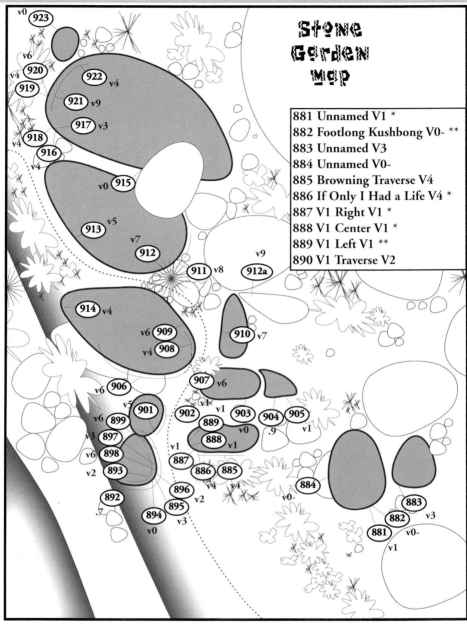

Stone
Garden
Map

881 Unnamed V1 *
882 Footlong Kushbong V0- **
883 Unnamed V3
884 Unnamed V0-
885 Browning Traverse V4
886 If Only I Had a Life V4 *
887 V1 Right V1 *
888 V1 Center V1 *
889 V1 Left V1 **
890 V1 Traverse V2

891 V1 Reverse V1
892 Breezy .7
893 Jacks Traverse V2 *
894 Brain Teaser V0
895 Kranium L V3 *
896 Kranium C V2/3
897 Kranium R V3 *

898 Misfire V6 **
899 Evolution V6 **
900 Greased Pig Var. V4
901 Intruder V5 **
902 Another Stupid Traverse V1
903 Unnamed V0
904 Unnamed .9

The Briar Patch Map p232

881 Unnamed V1 * Climbs a vertical face with nice patina edges.

882 Footlong Kushbong V0- ** Nice patina edges and knobs.

883 Unnamed V3 Sit start and climb the short overhang on gritty plates.

884 Unnamed V0- Crack, patina plates and knobs.

V1 Boulder Probably the first lines to go up at The Underground.
Good warm up. Map p232

885 Browning Traverse V4 A 30 ft. traverse along a juggy, horizontal crack with a pumpy finish.

886 If Only I Had a Life V4 * Sit start at the arête and pull thin crimps, slightly right, up the vertical face.

887 V1 Right V1 * Start at incuts 4 ft. up, move left to a hollow plate, then up to sweet jugs.

888 V1 Center V1 * Start at the low incuts and move straight up the knobby crack.

889 V1 Left V1 ** Start at the low incuts and move left out the corner of the roof to a jug , finishing on jugs.

890 V1 Traverse V2 Start on a jug, traverse right under the roof and finish on V1 right.

891 V1 Reverse V1 Start at the incuts, traverse left under the roof, finishing up the face.

Kranium Bloc Map p232

892 Breezy .7 Incut plates and flakes.

893 Jack's Traverse V2 * A 40 ft. traverse starting at Breezy, climbing high on the boulder and traversing along the lip at the overhanging finish. Pull over just before the two boulders intersect, of finish with the pumpy Greased Pig Var.

894 Brain Teaser V0 Start right hand on the incut flake, left on the arête. Pull up to pointy jugs and over.

895 Kranium L V3 * Start at a hueco/ledge, move left to a thin flake, then fire up to pointy jugs.

896 Kranium C V2/3 Start at the hueco/ledge, crank straight up to the lip.

897 Kranium R V3 * Start at the hueco/ledge, move right along a slotted seam, then up.

**898 Misfire V6 ** ** Sit start inside the bowl. Gaston/pinch the undersides of the bowl, fire out to the jug, then finish Kranium R.

**899 Evolution V6 ** ** 50 ft. traverse. Start at Breezy, traverse the middle of the face to a horizontal seam. Follow the seam around the corner to jugs, climb Kranium Right and finish Greased Pig.

900 Greased Pig Var. V4 Climb Jack's Traverse but continue under the two boulders and onto the ramp.

901 Intruder V5 ** Sit start at a large flake and crank right out the short 50° hang on incut flakes.

902 Another Stupid Traverse V1 Sit start and traverse left along the juggy lip 12 ft.

903 Unnamed V0 Sit start and climb the odd overhanging arête. Weird landing.

904 Unnamed .9 A short, vertical patina face.

905 Kilroy Was Here V1 Sit start on the left side of the small cave and pull small flakes up a clean face.

906 Altered States V6 R ***** Sit start at a pinch/match, Climb crazy incut plates on a 30° overhanging arête up to a large round patina jug, then moves over a large boulder for a closer landing, up to a long jug/plate (25 ft. up), turn onto patina and up the slab.

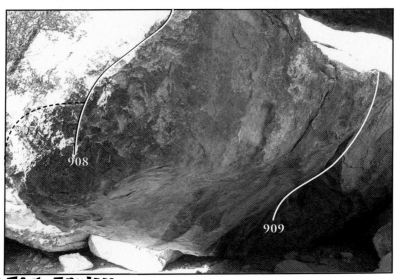

Zen Rock Garden

(GPS = N34° 03.579 W116° 06.152) A stoney place to chill. Map p232

907 Shock the Monkey V6 Sit start at Altered States and traverse right
around the corner to thin flakes and slopers, finishing matched on the
"head" sloper.

908 Delta Nova V4
Climb sharp, thin flakes up to
slopers.

909 Presence V6 ***
Sit start and power up into
sweet jams on polished
granite out an 8 ft. roof to a
juggy lip.

910 Damage Inc. V7 *
Sit start on the left side of a
large roof hueco, climb up
onto a vertical face with
micro edges.

**911 Zen Rock Garden
Traverse V8 ******
A 40 ft. traverse with
interesting moves. Sit start on
sloping chunks, traverse right
on a steep, shiny smooth lip.
Drop under the roof and into
unusual stems, finishing with
another steep, shiny smooth
(relentless) lip.

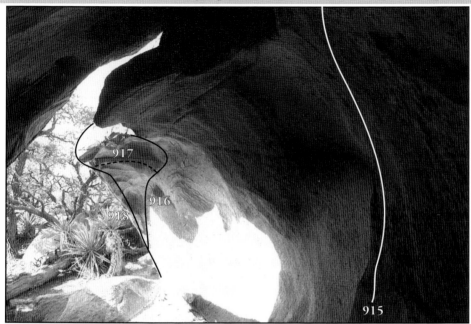

912 Zen Direct V7 ** Sit start on sloping chunks, traverse the sloping shelf to the roof, mantel onto the slab using the vertical wall.

912a Orange Tags V9 ** Sit start at edges and move left to a very steep arete.

913 Future Testpiece V5 *
Start at the lowest rail and pull the lip of the large roof.

914 4:20 V4 ***
Start low at the base of a 1 ft. thick sloping flake under a roof. Fire out the studded roof flake, turn the lip into a dihedral filled with patina goodness.

Porcelean Wall Map p232

915 The Hull V0 * Surreal granite.

916 Bodyglove V4 ***
Thoroughly entertaining. Sit start Body and Soul arête, move right and stem the concave face up to the ledge, traverse right and out the roof to jugs, mantel the 6 in. thick roof.

917 JB. Var. V3 * Stem up concave face to rail, traverse left joining Body and Soul.

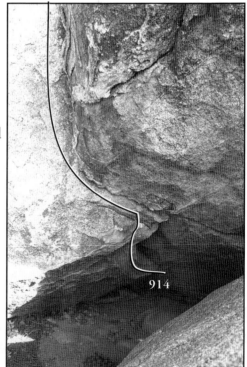

918 Body and Soul V5 ****
Sit start at an incut sidepull,
climb the steep, black arête to
balancy finish moves. Excellent
stone!

919 Slab Classic V4 ** Start at a
diagonal seam on a slab over a
low roof. A powerful mantel
gets you onto this clean, glassy
slab. Better holds high up.

920 Roof to Slab Classic V6 ***
Sit start at a large flake under
the roof. Fire the roof and pull
onto the slab, finishing on slab
classic.

921 Xenophobe V9 **** Sit start
at a large flake under the roof
traverse left along the lip of the
roof on hein slopers to a huge
tongue/jugs. Finish the upper
arête called Awkward Instant.

922 Awkward Instant V4 *
Start at jugs 6 ft. up on the lip of a roof. Perform awkward moves up
and left to the arête, loose plates above.

923 Unnamed V0 A short rounded buttress.

924 Divine Intervention V4 ***	941 Hueco Problem V2 ***
925 Divine Intervention(sit) V5 ***	942 Whiskey Tango V1
926 Rain Gutter V1	943 Aggro Fly V5 **
927 Ramskull Roof V3 *	944 The Golden Nugget V4 ***
928 Ramskull Direct V0-	945 Unnamed V0*
929 Unnamed V2	946 Unnamed V2**
930 Unnamed V2	947 Unnamed V1*
931 Unnamed .8	948 Unnamed V0
932 Runt V0	949 Unnamed V1
933 Moonstone V1	950 Unnamed V3 *
934 Pimp'in V7 **	951 Unnamed .7
935 Stone Raider V6 *	952 Lieback Crack V0
936 Browning Lip V5 *	953 Gutterbitch V0
937 Boldering .8	954 Corner V0
938 Browning Roof V4 **	955 Immaculate Perception V2 ***
939 Traverse of Morality V4 ***	956 Warm Up Problem V2 *
940 Unnamed V1	957 Feature Problem V3/4 ***

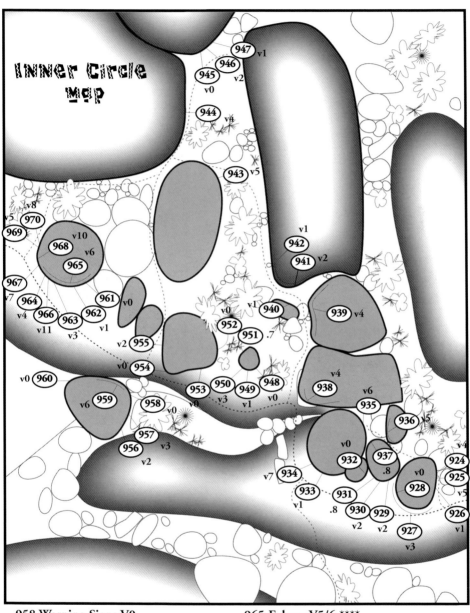

958 Warning Signs V0
959 Nicole Face V6 ***
960 If Its Browning, Flush-It V0 R
961 When Pigs Fly V0+
962 Saucer Full of Secrets V1 **
963 Ice Capades V3 **
964 Sketch V4 **

965 Echoes V5/6 ****
966 Blackfeet V11 ***
967 Doesn't Matter V7 ****
968 Dark Matter V10 *****
969 Eclipse V5 ****
970 Total Eclipse V8 ****

Divine Boulder Map p239

924 Divine Intervention V4 * Start on incut flakes on a hanging arête/bulge climb immaculate granite up to a horizontal crack and over.

925 Divine Intervention(sit) V5 * Sit start under the roof on thin crimps, traverse right 8 ft. on dope flakes.

926 Rain Gutter V1 Loose plates up a 16 ft. tall face with a hard deck landing.

927 Ramskull Roof V3 * Traverse along the jug laden lip of a roof for 30 ft. or so. Pull over when it gets slabby.

928 Ramskull Direct V0- Juggz on the lip of a roof to a vertical, plated face.

929 Unnamed V2 Sit start in the pit and traverse left on overhanging plates to jugs.

930 Unnamed V2 Sit start and climb the steep nose to jugs.

931 Unnamed .8 Patina plates and flakes.

932 Runt V0 Sit start at a low shelf and pull the low roof to a cruxy mantel.

Moonstone
Map p239

933 The Moonstone V1 Knobby patina flakes and plates.

934 Pimp'in V7 ** Sit start at the"hueco" like crimpers, Climb the bulging, velvety wall with small dimples and knobs.

935 Stone Raider V6 * Sit start at thin flakes under the roof and punch out to the sloping rail.

936 Browning Lip V5 * Sit start on the far right and traverse left along the lip of the overhang for 25 ft. or so.

937 Boldering .8 Patina plates up a rounded arete.

938 Browning Roof V4 **
Sit start off the boulder, down inside the roof, climb the roof with buckets to the knobby lip, then traverse right on the slab.

Hueco Corridor Map p239

939 Traverse of Morality V4 ***
A 30 ft. traverse starting with plates, then moving into water polished slopers, pockets, and seams. Technical moves. Finishes at a huge block.

940 Unnamed V1
A small slab problem.

941 Hueco Problem V2 ***
Climb juggy hueco's up to a smooth headwall 15 ft. up with small edges. Traverse left 6 ft. and downclimb.

942 Whiskey Tango V1 Traverse 30 ft. right along a juggy crack finishing at The Hueco Problem. Bad landing.

943 Aggro Fly V5 ** Squeeze the hanging lip and climb 5 ft. along the roof to thin incut flakes, up to a big ledge.

Secret Meadow Map p239

944 The Golden Nugget V4 *** Technical, vertical climbing on golden smooth patina. Climb a large plate to a horizontal crack high up.

945 Unnamed V0 * Patina slab.

946 Unnamed V2 ** Climb up a faint hueco/dish with balancy moves.

947 Unnamed V1 * Balance moves up a patina slab.

The Egg Map p239

948 Unnamed V0 Start at a huge jug and pull the egg shaped boulder.

949 Unnamed V1 From edges move up and right to join #948

950 Unnamed V3 * From edges move up and left to a vertical rail.

951 Unnamed .7 Short slab problem.

Immaculate Perception Boulder Map p239

952 Lieback Crack V0 The large flake/crack.

953 Gutterbitch V0 R Climb loose plates and buckets up a 20 ft. tall face. Sloped landing.

955

951

954 Corner V0 Start at jugs on the lip of a low roof up to a plated face.

955 Immaculate Perception V2 R * ** Climbs a 20 ft. tall vertical wall with technical edges to jugs higher up.

Feature Boulder Map p239

**956 Warm Up Problem V2 * ** Sit to start this short, steep jug haul.

957 Feature Problem V3/4 * ** Start as low as possible and climb steep incut plates up to jugs 20 ft. out.

958 Warning Signs V0 Climb rotten plates up this 22 ft. tall buttress to a huge jug. Bad landing.

959 Nicole Face V6 * ** A long crimp problem starting low on an arête, then climbing up, left, then up again on incut plates.

960 If Its Browning, Flush-It V0 R Climb patina knobs and jugs on the edge of a cliff.

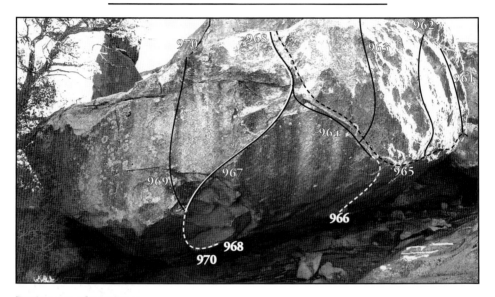

Eclipse Boulder Map p239

961 When Pigs Fly V0+ Short bulge with incut flakes.

962 Saucer Full of Secrets V1 ** Bulge with incut flakes to a dish and slopers.

963 Ice Capades V3 **Start along the juggy rail, move right on slopers and thin edges.

964 Sketch V4 ** Start on the right side of the juggy rail traverse left, following the thin crack to more jugs.

965 Echoes V5/6 **** Start at When Pigs Fly and traverse left along the lip, finishing with Sketch. Bomber incut flakes.

966 Blackfeet V11 *** Start under the roof on a large flake, punch out to the juggy rail and finish Sketch.

967 Doesn't Matter V7 **** Start at an undercling/jug 7 ft. up on the lip of the roof, traverse right and up to sloping rails.

968 Dark Matter V10 ***** Sit start at a 1 ft. thick sloping, dimpled out flake. Climb out the roof to join and finish with Does'nt Matter. This may be the finest problem in Joshua Tree.

969 Eclipse V5 **** Start at an undercling/jug 7 ft. up on the lip of the roof, move up and slightly left on the vertical upper face to a large dish and a jug at the 16 ft. level.

970 Total Eclipse V8 **** Sit start at the large dimpled flake, fire the roof and then finish with Eclipse.

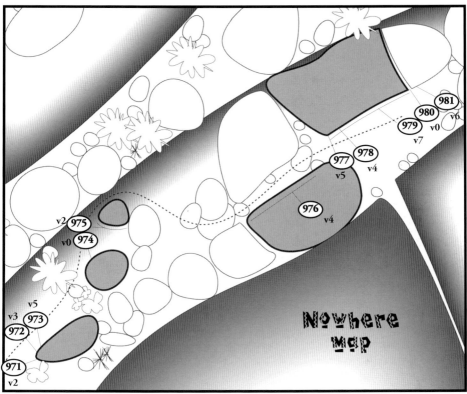

Nowhere
Map

971 Third Stone from the Sun V2 ***
972 Unnamed V3 ***
973 40° Wall V5 ****
974 Kamp Krusty V0
975 BFE V2 **
976 Darkpath Traverse V4 **

977 Have a Cigar V5 ****
978 Browning Escape V4
979 Hot Rats V7 ****
980 Hargis Offwidth V0
981 Freedom V6 *

40° Wall Map p245

971 Third Stone from the Sun V2 * ** Start at the thin holds on the arête, move up and right into the plated corner.

972 Unnamed V3 * ** Start at thin holds on the arête and climb the juggy arête left.

973 40° Wall V5 ** ** Start on thin holds on the arête. Climb left and up

on incut flakes, up 20 ft. to the "sharks tooth" jug. Arete on right off.

974 Kamp Krusty V0
Start at a high sidepull up to a horizontal crack and jugs.

975 BFE V2 **
Sit start and climb left along a juggy lip to huge jugs over a roof.

Browning Corridor

Shimmy past the BFE Boulder, climb over a boulder and into the low corridor. Map p245

976 Darkpath Traverse V4 ** Traverse 15 ft. right on a sloping, studded shelf to an arête with tight slopers. Rock right of the split off.

977 Have a Cigar V5 **** Sit start way under the roof at a small shelf, crank the long flake to its end and bomb straight out the prow to jugz. Finish up the 20 ft. tall arête.

978 Browning Escape V4

979 Hot Rats V7 **** Sit start at the obvious flat rail, traverse 15 ft. on excellent, small crimps to join Have a Cigar for the topout.

980 Hargis Offwidth V0 The overhanging offwidth.

981 Freedom V6 * Sit start in the "pit", climb flat jugs and crimps up and left. Finishes at the Hargis Offwidth.

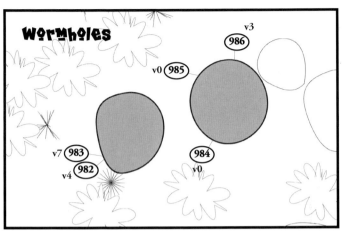

982 Goolsby Problem V4 *

983 Mulligan Variation V7 *

984 Browning Mantel V0

985 Unnamed V0

986 Unnamed V3 **

Wormholes Map p247

**982 Goolsby Problem V4 ***Climb the technical face above the cave on glassy patina knobs and flakes.

**983 Mulligan Variation V7 ***Sit start on the right side of the cave and traverse right into the goolsby problem.

984 Browning Mantel V0 Mantel onto the giant flake/crack.

985 Unnamed V0 The high crack.

986 Unnamed V3 ** Sit start and climb overhanging criss-cross cracks and out the bulge at the top.

Photo: R. Miramontes

Aron Couzens climbing Psyche

Chapter 21

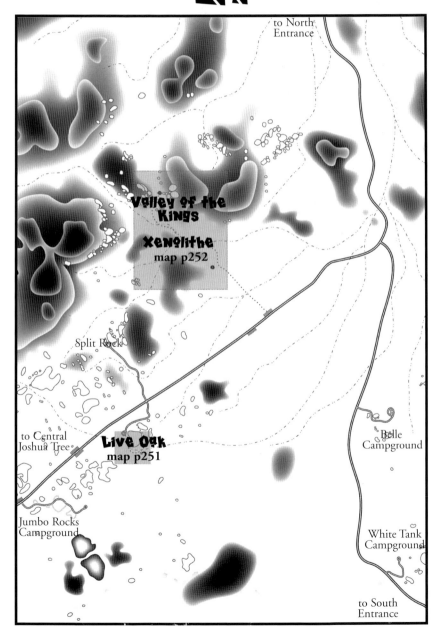

Eastern

Territories

As our final journey takes us through the Eastern most bouldering in the park, the formations become further and further apart. As the high plateau drops away, it gives way to a new landscape, a new frontier. This final area has much bouldering potential, the surface barely scratched as this book is written.

Must-do's in this area are the 35 ft. splitter roof crack Big Bob's Big Wedge, the exciting prow Psyche, and the the elegant line Alexandria.

Live Oak

This picnic area is located on the South side of Park Boulevard, approx. 10 miles from the North Entrance. Map p249, 251

The Xenolithe

From the Live Oak turnoff, drive East on Park Boulevard for approx. 2 miles, park at a paved turnout on the left side, about 20 ft. West of the turnout is a faint dirt road that heads towards the mountain, follow it. When the road drops down into the wash, go left back up the wash for 200 yds. Map p249, 252

Valley of the Kings

Follow the old dirt road into the wash, turn right and go into a huge wash, follow the trail around left (past the remains of a miners house)and walk through the sandy canyon, stay to the right and climb over a small impass. The canyon opens up and the wash will make a left bend at the hill, follow the wash for another 50 yds. and angle right over the small hill, at the top of the small hill you will see a large boulder on the right, walk right past the boulder and up the gully, The Mastaba is on the left. Past the top of the gully angle left and walk into the opening valley, The Rosetta Stone should be visible to the left. Map p249, 252

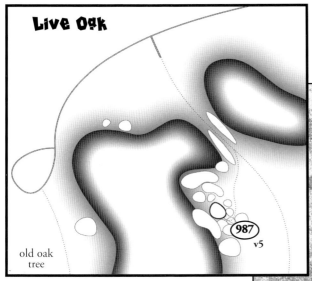

Live Oak

987
v5

old oak
tree

Big Bob's Big Wedge

(GPS = N33° 59.986 W116° 03.086)
Walk through the notch between the
two formations, look for a short bolt
route on a large boulder on the right.
Big Bob's Big Wedge is on the back
left side of this boulder.

987 Big Bobs Big Wedge V5 ***

Climbs a 30ft. splitter hand to fist
roof crack finishing with a brutal
offwidth at the lip.

978

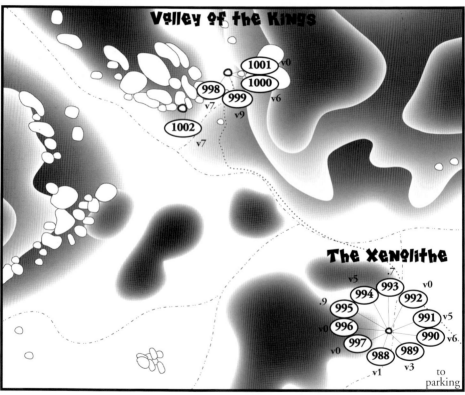

987 Big Bobs Big Wedge V5 ***
988 Typical Browning Death Slab V1 *
989 Lotus Flower V3 ***
990 Psyche V4 R ****
991 Xenolithic Var. V5 ***
992 Browning Slab R V0 *
993 Greenhorn Route .7 **
994 Email V5

995 Unnamed .9
996 Unnamed V0
997 Unnamed V0
998 Alexandria V7 R *****
999 The River Nile V9 R ***
1000 The Rosetta Stone V6 R ****
1001 Chapel of Osirus V0 **
1002 The Mastaba V7

The Xenolithe

(GPS = N34° 01.023 W116° 02.525) Map p252

988 Typical Browning Death Slab V1 *
Climb off the large boulder onto the rounded buttress with thin and sometimes loose plates. Bad landing.

989 Lotus Flower V3 **
Start at unusual hueco's and traverse right 15 ft. on gorgeous buckets, angling slightly up and finishing the same as Psyche.

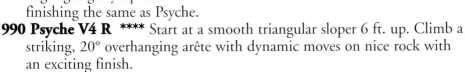

990 Psyche V4 R **** Start at a smooth triangular sloper 6 ft. up. Climb a striking, 20° overhanging arête with dynamic moves on nice rock with an exciting finish.

991 Xenolithic Var. V5 ** Sit start at an undercling edge on the left side of the small cave, traverse 8 ft. right on thin edges to the starting hold of Psyche, finishing the tall arête line.

992 Browning Slab R V0 * Climbs a smooth slab up to a headwall with a few ok holds. 20 ft.

993 Greenhorn Route .7 **
Climbs a 25 ft. low angle face/arete with beautiful patina plates.

994 Email V5
995 Unnamed .9
996 Unnamed V0
997 Unnamed V0

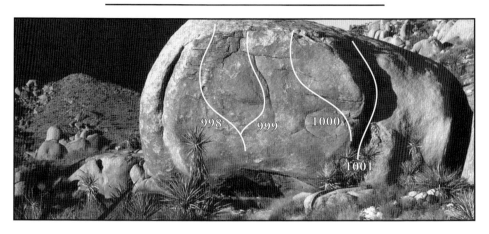

The Rosetta Stone

(GPS = N34° 01.543 W116° 02.939) Map p252

998 Alexandria V7 R ***** Climbs a 20 ft. vertical face on smooth cut edges and rails up a faint dike to sweet jugs. Jump off pads to first rail or pull static off micro crimps(**V8/9**).

999 The River Nile V9 R *** Start at Alexandria and traverse right, into the flaring, sketchy crack.

1000 The Rosetta Stone V6 R **** Start at Chapel of Osirus, traverse left on diagonal cracks to a crux dyno at the top.

1001 Chapel of Osirus V0 ** Climb the juggy, 20 ft. tall dike.

1002 The Mastaba V7 Traverse along a dike system.

Section 4

Indexes

VO

v1

v2

──────── **v4** ────────

Aguille de Joshua Tree (GPS = N34° 00.864 W116° 10.681)
Alisters Cave (GPS = N34° 01.913 W116° 09.007)
Arrowhead (GPS = N33° 59.016 W116° 09.081)
Asphalt Boulder (GPS = N34° 02.520 W116° 05.553)
Asteroid, The (GPS = N34° 00.712 W116° 09.072)
Beak Rock (GPS = N34° 01.453 W116° 09.334)
Betty Joe (GPS = N34° 00.746 W116° 10.114)
Big Bob's Big Wedge (GPS = N33° 59.986 W116° 03.086)
Big Brother Boulder (GPS = N33° 00.026 W116° 08.804)
Big Bud (GPS = N34° 01.207 W116° 10.989)
Big Dike (GPS = N34° 01.521 W116° 09.412)
Big Tree Boulder (GPS = N34° 02.479 W116° 05.521)
Black Velvet Boulder (GPS = N34° 00.572 W116° 10.120)
Blas Bimmer Boulder (GPS = N34° 01.671 W116° 10.725)
Blues Rock (GPS = N33° 56.859 W116° 04.714)
Boogie Nights (GPS = N34° 02.880 W116° 05.820)
Boulder of Noon (GPS = N34° 01.036 W116° 09.667)
Broken Boulder (GPS = N34° 02.409 W116° 11.627)
Broken Egg (GPS = N34° 00.665 W116° 10.037)
Campsite Grotto (GPS = N34° 01.027 W116° 09.638)
Caveman (GPS = N34° 00.975 W116° 09.795)
Cheese Boulder (GPS = N34° 01.536 W116° 10.755)
Chicken Wing (GPS = N34° 01.610 W116° 08.463)
Chip Flakey (GPS = N34° 00.865 W116° 09.651)
Chocolate Boulders(GPS = N34° 03.755 W116° 13.584)
Chube, The (GPS = N34° 01.705 W116° 08.718)
Chuckawalla Boulder (GPS = N34° 01.242 W116° 09.905)
Cilley Boulder (GPS = N33° 59.874 W116° 08.908)
Classic Thin Crack (GPS = N34° 01.517 W116° 09.530)
Coke Machine (GPS = N34° 00.739 W116° 09.751)
Colliherb (GPS = N33° 59.324 W116° 09.749)
Copper Penny (GPS = N34° 01.001 W116° 09.702)
Coyote Corner (GPS = N34° 01.520 W116° 09.658)
Deck, The (GPS = N34° 01.119 W116° 10.269)
Digitalis Destructi (GPS = N34° 00.587 W116° 10.156)
Dike Boulder (GPS = N33° 56.559 W116° 04.618)
Dike Boulder (GPS = N34° 01.113 W116° 09.939)
Discount Dyno (GPS = N34° 00.652 W116° 10.092)
Dripper Boulder (GPS = N33° 56.806 W116° 04.356)
Dwarf (GPS = N33° 59.849 W116° 08.786)
Egghead (GPS = N34° 00.608 W116° 09.911)